THE MONSTROUS R...
A Book of Aphorisms

The Monstrous Regiment is a highly entertaining collection of aphorisms on the subject of women which will fascinate both members and observers of the Women's Movement.

From Nietzche's outrageous 'When a woman becomes a scholar, there is usually something wrong with her sex organs' to Wordsworth's magisterial 'A perfect woman, nobly planned/To warn, to comfort and command' we experience here the whole gamut of male response to women.

We hear from women too – the cool, clear voice of Jane Austen: 'It is always incomprehensible to a man that a woman should refuse an offer of marriage' – the robust common sense of George Eliot: 'I am not denying women are foolish: God Almighty made 'em to match the men' – and the passionate cry of a twentieth-century feminist: 'If men could get pregnant, abortion would be a sacrament'.

The selection of more than a thousand of the pithiest sayings about the sexes also includes some of the truest compliments ever paid to either.

Elegantly arranged in eighteen thematic chapters, *The Monstrous Regiment* is a rich harvest of wisdom, prejudice, benignity and rage.

Thirty-year-old Margaret Blackwood who lives in Victoria, Canada, has worked on various literary projects – most recently co-authorship (with Robin Skelton) of *Earth, Air, Fire, Water* which traces the Pagan elements in the poetry of the British Isles.

THE MONSTROUS REGIMENT

A Book of Aphorisms

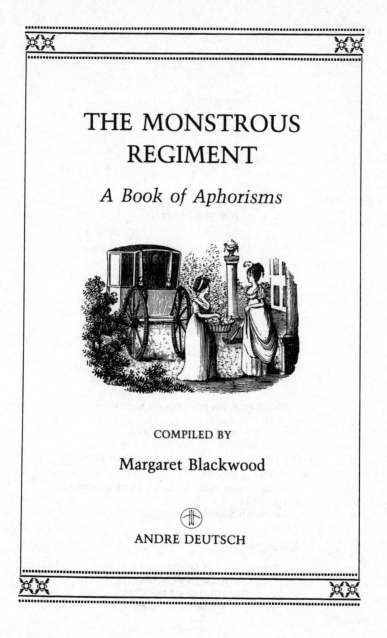

COMPILED BY

Margaret Blackwood

ANDRE DEUTSCH

FOR MY PARENTS

FIRST PUBLISHED 1990 BY
ANDRE DEUTSCH LIMITED
105-106 GREAT RUSSELL STREET, LONDON WC1B 3LJ

BRITISH LIBRARY CATALOGUING IN PUBLICATION DATA
THE MONSTROUS REGIMENT.
   1. QUOTATIONS IN ENGLISH. SPECIAL SUBJECTS: WOMEN –
   ANTHOLOGIES
   I. BLACKWOOD, MARGARET
   808.882

ISBN 0 233 98582 4

PHOTOTYPESET BY FALCON GRAPHIC ART LTD
WALLINGTON, SURREY
PRINTED IN GREAT BRITAIN BY
WBC Print Ltd., Bridgend

Contents

৯

There will always remain something to be said of women, as long as there is one on the earth.

Jean, Chevalier de Boufflers

Preface

To be successful, an aphorism doesn't necessarily have to be truthful, but it should leave one with that impression. As W.H. Auden and Louis Kronenberger state in their *Faber Book of Aphorisms* (1964), an aphorism 'must convince every reader that it is either universally true or true of every member of the class to which it refers, irrespective of the reader's convictions'. Additionally, there are no set rules as to length, but aphorisms should be punchy and direct in style. They are often highly opinionated, and frequently contradict each other, even when written by the same hand. Along with the deliberate aphorisms in this book, there are excerpts from poetry, prose and letters, and while these may not have been intended as aphorisms originally, they do seem to have the qualities required of the form.

In the light of today's concerns, however, it is hardly possible to find a resounding truth in every one of the aphorisms included here. At the same time as there are striking, often thought-provoking, opinions, there are humorous, if not ludicrous and dated, examples of the attitudes that various authors and public figures – male and female alike – have held about women over the years.

This book is intended to demonstrate to both members and observers of the women's movement exactly what has been said about women through the centuries, but reverence and ribaldry, prejudice and percipience, rub shoulders here. Some of these aphorisms are, quite simply, outrageous. Nietzsche's 'When a woman becomes a scholar there is usually something wrong with her sexual organs', for instance, was absurd even in its own time; whereas Euripides'

'Families can ill spare a man [by death]; women are not such a loss', while not applicable today, could be read as a glimpse into the hardships faced by the society of the author's time.

While some aphorisms are obviously meant to be amusing, such as the anonymous entry, 'An old coquette does not die of old age — she dies of anxiety', and John Barrymore's 'The way to fight a woman is with your hat. Grab it and run', others take an ironic approach, such as H.L. Mencken's 'Love is the delusion that one woman differs from another'. Others still, are anything but humorous, such as 'There's no human being a man can buy anymore — except a woman' by Clare Boothe Luce, and Nietzsche's poignant 'Woman was God's second mistake'.

Needless to say, compiling this book was an eye-opening experience. Not only did I discover new sources as it grew, but patterns began to emerge. It became apparent that some aphorisms had been written as a consequence of others. There is little doubt, for instance, that Cyril Connolly's 'There is no fury like a woman searching for a new lover' is based on Congreve's well known 'Heav'n has no rage . . . / Nor Hell a fury, like a woman scorn'd'. Equally, it could be true that Dorothy Parker's 'Women and elephants never forget' comes from Saki's 'Women and elephants never forget an injury'.

To include here every aphoristic statement ever written about women would be virtually impossible. The sources alone are endless. In fact, I am sure that even by settling for over a thousand entries I have still only managed to skim the surface. I have attempted, however, to include a fair representation from each century, and hope that I have provided at least an overview of the subject.

I have tried to remain neutral as well, but the nature of aphorisms makes them difficult to collect without a certain degree of bias. For this reason, and for purposes of perspective, the book has been arranged thematically, and chronologically, within sections. In the interest of fair play, I have also included a section about men.

Lastly, and with affection, I would like to thank Robin Skelton, for without his friendship and provocation this book would never have come to mind.

M.B.

Intellect

You ask whether woman possesses any natural intelligence. Yes. It can be developed to become wisdom, and then it is most beautiful.

Christine de Pisan

There is no gown or garment that worse becomes a woman than when she will be wise.

Martin Luther

A woman's thought runs before her actions.

*

Men have marble, women waxen minds.

William Shakespeare

Women are most fools when they think they're wisest.

Beaumont and Fletcher

Women ought not to know their own wit, because they will still be showing it, and so spoil it.

John Selden

... There's naught
That's more unsteadfast than a woman's thought.

John Cooke

One tongue is sufficient for a woman.

*Attrib. John Milton
when asked to teach his
daughters foreign languages*

A learned woman is thought to be a comet, that bodes mischief whenever it appears.

*

Let women be fools, and then you may easily make them slaves.

Bathsua Makin

The intellect of the greater part of women serves more to strengthen their folly than their reason.

La Rochefoucauld

Women's minds are like shops of small-wares, wherein some have pretty toys, but nothing of any great value.

Margaret Cavendish

... a woman in this age is considered learned enough if she can distinguish her husband's bed from that of another.

Hannah Wooley

What has poor woman done, that she must be debar'd from sense, and sacred poetry?

Aphra Behn

Wit is more necessary than beauty; and I think no young woman ugly that has it, and no handsome woman agreeable without it.

William Wycherley

Alas! a woman that attempts the pen,
Such an intruder on the rights of men,
Such a presumptuous creature, is esteemed,
The fault can by no vertue be redeemed.

Anne Finch

The woman that deliberates is lost.

Joseph Addison

... you can come into no company of Ladies and Gentlemen, where you shall not hear an open and Vehement exclamation against Learned Women.

Elizabeth Elstob

Women especially are to be talked to as below men, and above children.

Lord Chesterfield

A woman's preaching is like a dog's walking on his hinder legs. It is not done well; but you are surprised to find it done at all.

*

A man is in general better pleased when he has a good dinner upon his table, than when his wife talks Greek.

Dr Johnson

The world is the book of women. Whatever knowledge they may possess is more commonly acquired by observation than by reading.

Jean-Jacques Rousseau

The charms of women were never more powerful – never inspired such achievements, as in those immortal periods, when they could neither read nor write. *Hannah Cowley*

A woman, especially if she have the misfortune of knowing anything, should conceal it as well as she can.

Jane Austen

Women never reason, and therefore they are (comparatively) seldom wrong.

*

His sayings are generally like women's letters; all the pith is in the postscript. *William Hazlitt, of Charles Lamb*

Wherever you go, you will hear all around:
The wisdom of woman to the distaff is bound.

Rahel Morpurgo

Intellectual women are the most modest inquirers after truth, and accomplished women often the most scrupulous observers of social duty. *Bronson Alcott*

The brain-women never interest us like the heart-women; white roses please less than red. *Oliver Wendell Holmes*

Woman's pleasure, woman's pain –
Nature made them blinder motions bounded in a shallower brain. *Alfred, Lord Tennyson*

4

A woman's best qualities do not reside in her intellect, but in her affections. She gives refreshment by her sympathies, rather than by her knowledge.

Samuel Smiles

. . . woman's discontent increases in exact proportion to her development.

Elizabeth Cady Stanton

Woman is quick to recognize genius, and to listen when wisdom speaks. – She may chatter in the presence of fools, but knows and appreciates the value of earnest, sensible men.

Caroline H. Dall

Women's thoughts are impelled by their feelings. Hence the sharp-sightedness, the direct instinct, the quick perceptions, hence also their warmer prejudices and more unbalanced judgements . . . In this the child is like the woman.

Antoinette Brown Blackwell

. . . a learned woman is the greatest of all calamities.

Baroness Marie von Ebner-Eschenbach

When a woman becomes a scholar there is usually something wrong with her sexual organs.

Friedrich Nietzsche

A woman who is confuted is never convinced.

John Churton Collins

[Woman] is quick to revere genius, but in her secret soul she seldom loves it.

Agnes Repplier

The less a woman has in her head the better she is for climbing.
Olive Schreiner

Women's rougher, simpler, more upright judgement embraces the whole truth, which their tact, their mistrust of masculine idealism, ever prevents them from speaking in its entirety.
Joseph Conrad

An intelligent woman is a woman with whom we can be as stupid as we like.
Paul Valéry

A woman who thinks she is intelligent demands equal rights with men. A woman who *is* intelligent does not.
Colette

Can you recall a woman who ever showed you with pride her library?
Benjamin de Cassères

Women are getting dumber as they grow smarter.
Mary Garden

Women seldom have the pathological faculty vaguely called imagination.

*

Women decide the larger questions of life correctly and quickly, not because they are lucky guessers, not because they are divinely inspired, not because they practise a magic inherited from savagery, but simply and solely because they have sense.
H.L. Mencken

6

Where a man takes up objective problems, a woman contents herself with solving riddles; where he battles for knowledge and understanding, she contents herself with faith or superstition, or else she makes assumptions.

Emma Jung

Women are wiser than men because they know less and understand more.

James Stephens

All observations point to the fact that the intellectual woman is masculinized; in her, warm, intuitive knowledge has yielded to cold unproductive thinking.

Helene Deutsch

Women are brighter than men. That's true. But it should be kept very quiet or it ruins the whole racket.

Anita Loos

Women never use their intelligence – except when they need to prop up their intuition.

Jacques Deval

It never pays to complicate a woman's mind too much.

Taylor Caldwell

A woman knows how to keep quiet when she is in the right, whereas a man, when he is in the right, will keep on talking.

Malcolm de Chazal

But if God had wanted us to think with our wombs, why did he give us a brain?

Clare Boothe Luce

The brightest of women are not bright.

Lillian Hellman

In general all curvaceousness strikes men as incompatible with the life of the mind.

Françoise Parturier

All women are the same. It's the intellect that counts.

Eric Rohmer

... we whose hands have rocked the cradle, are now using our heads to rock the boat ...

Wilma Scott Heide

A thinking woman sleeps with monsters.

Adrienne Rich

Sometimes I'm charmed by the fact that there are women with whom you can discuss the molecular theory of light all evening, and at the end they will ask you what is your birth sign.

Roman Polanski

Women never have young minds. They are born three thousand years old.

Shelagh Delaney

It's unfortunate that Hollywood could not visualize a woman of mental acumen unless she was fixing up a mess her man/boss had made, covering a scoop to prove herself to a man, or deftly forging a life of dishonesty.

Marjorie Rosen

The surest way to win the regard of a sensible woman is to treat her intellect with deferential respect – to talk to her as a thinking being.

*

The finest compliment that can be paid to a woman of sense is to address her as such.

Anon.

Vanity and Appearance

Manner, not gold, is woman's best adornment.

Menander

How wrong you are, woman, to have such confidence in your beauty.

Propertius

Every woman thinks herself attractive; even the plainest is satisfied with the charms she deems that she possesses.

Ovid

If a woman have long hair, it is a glory to her.

1 Corinthians 11:15

It is a high distinction for a homely woman to be loved for her character rather than for beauty.

*

When the candles are out all women are fair.

Plutarch

A woman's appearance depends upon two things: the clothes she wears and the time she gives to her toilet . . . Against the first we bring the charge of ostentation, against the second, of harlotry.   *Tertullian*

There is no torture that a woman would not endure to enhance her beauty.   *Montaigne*

Beauty, in a modest woman, is like fire, or a sharp sword at a distance: neither doth the one burn, nor the other wound those that come not too near them.   *Miguel de Cervantes*

A fair woman is a paradise to the eye, a purgatory to the purse, and a hell to the soul.   *Elizabeth Grymeston*

A woman mov'd is like a fountain troubled,
Muddy, ill-seeming, thick, bereft of beauty.

*

A woman is a dish for the gods, if the devil dress her not.

William Shakespeare

A woman, the more curious she is about her face, is commonly the more careless about her house.   *Ben Jonson*

And what shall we say otherwise of that baring of their necks, shoulders, naked breasts, arms and wrists? To what end are they but only to tempt men to lust?   *Robert Burton*

Shall I, wasting in despair,
    Die because a woman's fair?

George Wither

A beautiful woman should break her mirror early.

Baltasar Gracián

The severity of women is a contrivance and a sham which they add to their beauty.

*

There are few women whose merit outlives their beauty.

*

It is valueless to a woman to be young unless pretty, or to be pretty unless young.   *La Rochefoucauld*

If women were by nature what they make themselves by artifice, if their faces suddenly became as bright or as leaden as they make them with paint and powder, they would be inconsolable.

*

If a handsome woman allows that another woman is beautiful, we may safely conclude she excels her.

Jean de la Bruyère

No woman can be handsome by the force of features alone, any more than she can be witty only by the help of speech.

Richard Steele

Women were made to give our eyes delight.
A female sloven is an odious sight.

Edward Young

What woman can resist the force of praise?

John Gay

Women who are either indisputably beautiful or indisputably ugly are best flattered upon the score of their understandings.

Lord Chesterfield

Vanity ruins more women than love.

Marie du Deffand

A beautiful and sparkling, but superficial woman rules a wide circle; a woman of real culture a small one.

Johann Wolfgang von Goethe

. . . women's power seldom lasts longer than their complexion.

*

To be forsaken and ugly, are the greatest distresses a woman can have.

Elizabeth Inchbald

Young ladies are delicate plants. They should take care of their health and their complexion.

*

It is very hard that a pretty woman is never to be told she is so by any one of her own sex without that person's being suspected to be either her determined Enemy, or her professed Toadeater.

Jane Austen

13

Ladies grow handsome by looking at themselves in the glass.

*

A woman's vanity is interested in making the object of her choice the God of her idolatry.

William Hazlitt

Ladies of Fashion starve their happiness to feed their vanity, and their love to feed their pride.

Charles Colton

I hate a dumpy woman.

Lord Byron

This is always the way with you men; let a woman only be handsome, and you are already to pity her, whatsoever her transgressions may have been.

Marguerite Blessington

There are no ugly women; there are only women who do not know how to use cosmetics.

Attrib. Pierre Antoine Berryer

I have heard with admiring submission the experience of the lady who declared that the sense of being well-dressed gives a feeling of inward tranquillity, which religion is powerless to bestow.

*

A beautiful woman is a practical poet.

Ralph Waldo Emerson

Women never look so well as when one comes in wet and dirty from hunting.

R.S. Surtees

A woman may be ugly, ill-shaped, wicked, ignorant, and stupid, but hardly ever ridiculous.

Louis Desnoyers

14

The wisest woman you talk with is ignorant of something that you know, but an elegant woman never forgets her elegance.

Oliver Wendell Holmes

The beauty of a lovely woman is like music.

George Eliot

What a strange illusion it is to suppose that beauty is goodness! A beautiful woman utters absurdities: we listen, and we hear not the absurdities but wise thoughts.

Leo Tolstoy

Lovely female shapes are terrible complicators of the difficulties and dangers of this earthly life, especially for their owner.

George du Maurier

A thoroughly beautiful woman and a thoroughly homely woman are creations which I love to gaze upon, and which I cannot tire of gazing upon, for each is perfect in her own line.

Mark Twain

Women themselves always still have in the background of all personal vanity an impersonal contempt for 'woman'.

Friedrich Nietzsche

It is the prime duty of a woman of this terrestrial world to look well. Neatness is the asepsis of clothes.

Sir William Osler

There are only two kinds of women, the plain and the coloured.

*

I don't mind plain women being Puritans. It is the only excuse they have for being plain.

Oscar Wilde

Have you ever noticed ... that many jewels make women either incredibly fat or incredibly thin?

Sir J.M. Barrie

There are three things a woman ought to look — straight as a dart, supple as a snake, and proud as a tiger lily.

*

A lady, however poor, should wear fine linen — even if she can only have one new dress a year.

*

A combination of red hair, green eyes, and black eyelashes causes anxieties. It would do well with such a mixture to establish yourself early in life. Good girls don't have that colouring.

*

Women with the faces of angels are deuced dangerous folks at the best of times.

Elinor Glyn

When a woman ceases to alter the fashion of her hair, you guess that she has passed the crisis of her experience.

Mary Hunter Austin

There are no ugly women, only lazy ones.

Helena Rubinstein

A good many women are good-tempered simply because it saves the wrinkles coming too soon.

Baroness von Hutten

Some women are not beautiful — they only look as though they are.

*

A woman who cannot be ugly is not beautiful.

Karl Kraus

If a man hears much that a woman says, she is not beautiful.

Henry S. Haskins

From the day on which she weighs 140, the chief excitement of a woman's life consists in spotting women who are fatter than she is.

Helen Rowland

The average woman, until art comes to her aid, is ungraceful, misshapen, badly calved and crudely articulated, even for a woman.

*

The female body, even at its best, is very defective in form; it has harsh curves and very clumsily distributed masses; compared to it the average milk jug, or even cuspidor, is a thing of intelligent and gratifying design — in brief, an *objet d'art*.

*

No woman is ever offended by admiration.

H.L. Mencken

A pretty woman has the right to be ignorant of everything, provided she knows when to keep still.

Jean Giraudoux

Wearing her skirt half-way up the thigh does not give a woman the advantage.

Coco Chanel

No woman is a beauty to her maid.

*

There are only two crimes for women — fat and age.

Hildric Davenport

The expression a woman wears on her face is far more important than the clothes she wears on her back.

Dale Carnegie

As [a woman] gets older and older, the appearance becomes such a bore.

Enid Bagnold

Beauty's the thing that counts
In women; red lips
And black eyes are better than brains.

Mary J. Elmendorf

When a man confronts catastrophe on the road, he looks in his purse — but a woman looks in her mirror.

Margaret Turnbull

No woman can be too rich or too thin.

Attrib. Duchess of Windsor

A beauty is a woman you notice; a charmer is one who notices you.

Adlai Stevenson

Women always show more taste in their choice of under-clothing than in their choice of jewelry.

Malcolm de Chazal

Glamour is what makes a man ask for your telephone number. But it also is what makes a woman ask for the name of your dressmaker.

Lilly Daché

It matters more what's in a woman's face than what's on it.

Claudette Colbert

. . . plain women know more about men than beautiful ones do.

Katharine Hepburn

Without security it is difficult for a woman to look or feel beautiful.

Merle Oberon

In Britain, an attractive woman is somehow suspect.

Vivien Leigh

A real woman is a young, pretty, sexy, tender woman who is no taller than five feet six who adores you.

Françoise Parturier

I am told when surface beauty is gone, the real woman emerges.

Linda Darnell

The only place men want depth in a woman is in her *décolletage*.

Attrib. Zsa Zsa Gabor

The bikini was invented by a girl who didn't want men to notice the little red spots around her nose.

Jacques Languirand

The problem of fading beauty in a woman is one of the powerful themes not only of drama, but of life itself.

Claire Bloom

There are no really ugly women. Every woman is a Venus in her own way.

Brigitte Bardot

There is not one female comic who was beautiful as a little girl.

Joan Rivers

If proof were needed of the power of woman's film image on women in life, the number of platinum heads tells the story.

Marjorie Rosen

A girl with large breasts has two strikes against her.

Valerie Perrine

Look at a woman at night, from afar, or under an umbrella.

Japanese proverb

A well turned out woman is never ugly.

Spanish proverb

Choose neither a woman nor linen by candle-light.

*

A man is as old as he feels, and a woman as old as she looks.

*

We like a speech to be like a woman's dress: long enough to take in the principal part, yet short enough to make it interesting.

*

A woman's beauty is not a gift to man — only a bribe.

Anon.

Youth and Age

Old women should not seek to be perfumed.

Plutarch

The years that a woman subtracts from her age are not lost.
They are added to the ages of other women.

Attrib. Diane de Poitiers

Old, that's an affront no woman can well bear.

Miguel de Cervantes

Old age is woman's hell.

Ninon de Lenclos

The Devil's in her tongue, and so 'tis in most women's of her
age; for when it has quitted the tail, it repairs to the upper
tier.

Aphra Behn

If one wants to form an idea of the self-love of women in their youth, one has only to judge by how much remains to them when they are no longer of an age to be attractive.

Nicolas de Chamfort

But an old woman ... is a person who has no sense of decency; if once she takes to living, the devil himself can't get rid of her.

Fanny Burney

There are three classes into which all old women are divided: first, that dear old soul: second, that old woman; and third, that old witch.

Samuel Taylor Coleridge

A lady of a 'certain age', which means
Certainly aged.

Lord Byron

There is no such thing as an old woman. Any woman of any age, if she loves, if she is good, gives a man a sense of the infinite.

Jules Michelet

Few women, I fear, have had such reason as I have to think the long sad years of youth were worth living for the sake of middle age.

George Eliot

A man is as old as he's feeling,
A woman as old as she looks.

Mortimer Collins

A woman is as old as she looks before breakfast.

Edgar Watson Howe

23

No woman should ever be quite accurate about her age. It looks so calculating.

Oscar Wilde

A woman would rather visit her own grave than the place where she has been young and beautiful after she is aged and ugly.

Corra May Harris

I am not half as patient with old women now that I am one.

Emily Carr

Most women are not so young as they are painted.

Sir Max Beerbohm

Nothing ages a woman like living in the country.

Colette

Time and tide wait for no man, but time always stands still for a woman of thirty.

Robert Frost

A girl of fifteen generally has a greater number of secrets than an old man, and a woman of thirty more arcana than a chief of state.

José Ortega y Gasset

The nightingale sings many seasons; the rose blooms but one. Youth comes only once — to a woman.

Hildric Davenport

Time and trouble will tame an advanced young woman, but an advanced old woman is uncontrollable by any earthly force.

Dorothy L. Sayers

The British just can't believe that a woman over thirty-five can be sexy.

Honor Blackman

Women may be the one group that grows more radical with age.

Gloria Steinem

A woman is as young as her knee.

Mary Quant

Old women turn into old men.

Joyce Carol Oates

Both women and melons are best when fairly ripe.

Spanish proverb

A woman is an angel at ten, a saint at fifteen, a devil at forty and a witch at fourscore.

*

Women and music should never be dated.

*

An old coquette does not die of old age – she dies of anxiety.

Anon.

25

Temperament

Oh woman, woman! when to ill thy mind
Is bent, all hell contains no fouler fiend.

Homer

Neither earth nor ocean produces a creature as savage and monstrous as woman.

Euripides

A continual dropping in a very rainy day and a contentious woman are alike.

Proverbs 27:15

All wickedness is but little to the wickedness of a woman.

Ecclesiasticus

I know the disposition of women: when you will, they won't; when you won't, they set their hearts upon you of their own inclination.

Terence

A fickle and changeable thing is woman ever.

Virgil

Whether they give or refuse, women are glad to have been asked.

Ovid

Women one and all are a set of vultures.

Petronius

There's no effrontery like that of a woman caught in the act; her very guilt inspires her with wrath and insolence.

*

Never trust a woman so savage as when her hatred is goaded by shame.

Juvenal

I judge impetuosity to be better than caution; for Fortune is a woman, and if you wish to master her, you must strike and beat her.

Niccolò Machiavelli

All women are ambitious naturally.

Christopher Marlowe

Do you not know I am a woman? when I think, I must speak.

*

Oh, tiger's heart wrapped in a woman's hide!

*

Women are shrews, both short and tall.

*

'Tis said a woman's fitness comes by fits.

*

A woman's nay does stand for nought.

*

27

I have no other but a woman's reason:
I think him so, because I think him so.

William Shakespeare

Besides, I have a woman's reason, I will not dance, because I will not dance.

Thomas Middleton

. . . In wickedness,
The wit of woman was ne'er yet found barren.

Shackerley Marmion

The souls of women are so small,
That some believe they've none at all.

Samuel Butler

Had God intended women only as a finer sort of cattle, He would not have made them reasonable.

Bathsua Makin

Women do not know the extent of their coquetry.

*

There can be no control in the mind or heart of women unless their temperament is in accordance with it.

*

Coquettes make a point of being jealous of their lovers in order to conceal that they are envious of other women.

*

Coquetry is the foundation of the temperament of women but all do not put it into practice, because in some coquetry is restrained by fear or by reason.

*

Women are not entirely unkind without aversion.

*

28

Women are less able to overcome coquetry than passion.

La Rochefoucauld

... [as to] the most part of women being lyers, [it] is onely out of their goodnesses to cover the faults and abuses of men.

Mary Tattlewell

A woman's head is like the weathercock on the top of a house, which turns at the first breeze.

Molière

She wavers, she hesitates: in a word, she is a woman.

Jean Racine

Women are ever in extremes; they are either better or worse than men.

Jean de la Bruyère

The pleasure of talking is the inextinguishable passion of women, coeval with the act of breathing.

Alain-René Le Sage

Women are like tricks by slight of hand,
Which, to admire, we should not understand.

William Congreve

There would be no such animals as prudes or coquettes in the world were there not such an animal as man.

Joseph Addison

A jealous woman believes everything her passion suggests.

*

An inconstant woman, tho' she has no chance to be very happy, can never be very unhappy.

John Gay

No woman ever hates a man for being in love with her; but many a woman hates a man for being a friend to her.

*

Most women have no characters at all.

*

Woman's at best a contradiction still.

*

Men, some to business, some to pleasure take;
But every woman is at heart a rake.

Alexander Pope

Women are much more like each other than men: they have, in truth, but two passions, vanity and love.

Lord Chesterfield

You teach your daughters the diameters of the planets, and wonder when you have done that they do not delight in your company.

Dr Johnson

A cunning woman is a knavish fool.

George, Lord Lyttelton

Women are very pleased when you accuse them of being cruel.

Pierre-Augustin Caron de Beaumarchais

O! woman, woman! whether lean or fat,
In face an angel, but in soul a cat!

Peter Pindar

... if she is a true woman, her displeasure will rise in proportion to your contrition.

Hannah Cowley

Watch out for women's tricks.

Wolfgang Amadeus Mozart

Women are like thermometers, which on a sudden application of heat sink at first a few degrees, as a preliminary to rising a good many.

Jean Paul Richter

... women being the victims of all social institutions, are destined to misery if they make the least concession to their feelings and if, in any way whatever, they lose control of themselves.

Germaine de Staël

Women do not transgress the bounds of decorum so often as men; but when they do they go to greater lengths.

Charles Colton

Women are always eagerly on the lookout for any emotion.

Stendhal

But a woman's whole existence is a history of the affections.

Washington Irving

Woman is a creature without reason, who pokes fire from the top.

Archbishop Richard Whately

I have but one simile, and that's a blunder,
For wordless woman, which is silent thunder.

*

Sweet is revenge — especially to women.

*

Woman, thy vows are traced in sand.

Lord Byron

Women forgive injuries, but never forget slights.

*

Every woman is wrong until she cries, and then she is right, instantly.

Thomas C. Haliburton

I will not say that women have no character; rather, they have a new one every day.

Heinrich Heine

To our shame a woman is never so attached to us as when we suffer.

*

To feel, to love, to suffer, to devote herself will always be the text of the life of a woman.

Honoré de Balzac

A good cigar is as great a comfort to a man as a good cry is to a woman.

Edward George Bulwer-Lytton

Woman wronged, can cherish hate
More deep and dark than manhood may.

John Greenleaf Whittier

What hearts have men! they never mount
As high as woman in her selfless mood.

*

Men at most differ as heaven and earth; but women, worst and best, as heaven and hell.

Alfred, Lord Tennyson

A woman without a laugh in her . . . is the greatest bore in existence.
William Makepeace Thackeray

A woman forgives only when she is in the wrong.
Arsène Houssaye

Women wish to be loved without a why or a wherefore – not because they are pretty or good, or well-bred, or graceful, or intelligent, but because they are themselves.
Henri-Frédéric Amiel

Women never confess; even when they seemingly resign themselves to such a course, they are never sincere.
Émile Gaboriau

A woman springs a sudden reproach upon you which provokes a hot retort – and then she will presently ask you to apologize.
Mark Twain

Woman learns how to hate in the degree that she forgets how to charm.

*

In revenge and in love woman is more barbarous than man.
Friedrich Nietzsche

Women are always on the defensive.
John Churton Collins

The great question that has never been answered, and which I have not yet been able to answer despite my thirty years of research into the feminine soul is: What does a woman want?
Sigmund Freud

33

Nothing spoils a romance so much as a sense of humour in the woman.

*

Every woman is a rebel, and usually in wild revolt against herself.

*

There is nothing in the whole world so unbecoming to a woman as a Nonconformist conscience.

Oscar Wilde

Changeable women are more endurable than monotonous ones. They are sometimes murdered but seldom deserted.

George Bernard Shaw

Women love the lie that saves their pride, but never an unflattering truth.

Gertrude Franklin Atherton

A woman, like a cross-eyed man, looks one way, but goes another – hence her mysteriousness.

Austin O'Malley

A woman never sees what we do for her, she only sees what we don't do.

Georges Courteline

A woman's mind is cleaner than a man's – she changes it oftener.

Oliver Herford

Ladies do not like being called icebergs. Such remarks are always rude, and often incorrect.

Norman Douglas

Women like to sit down with trouble as if it were knitting.

Ellen Glasgow

Feminine passion is to masculine as an epic to an epigram.

Karl Kraus

34

A woman can forgive a man for the harm he does her, but she can never forgive him for the sacrifices he makes on her account.

*

A woman will always sacrifice herself if you give her the opportunity. It is her favourite form of self-indulgence.

W. Somerset Maugham

A capacity for self-pity is one of the last things that any woman surrenders.

Irvin S. Cobb

Women are like dogs really. They love like dogs, a little insistently. And they like to fetch and carry and come back wistfully after hard words, and learn rather easily to carry a basket.

Mary Roberts Rinehart

My vigor, vitality and cheek repel me. I am the kind of woman I would run away from.

Nancy Astor

The whole thing about the women is, they lust to be misunderstood.

Will Rogers

Pique has caused the downfall of more women than Love.

Walter Pulitzer

It is women who love horror. Gloat over it. Feed on it. Are nourished by it. Shudder and cling and cry out – and come back for more. Women have a predestination to suffering.

Bela Lugosi

It is interesting to note that in every phase of life feminine masochism finds some form of expression. *Helene Deutsch*

If a woman hasn't got a tiny streak of a harlot in her, she's a dry stick as a rule. *D.H. Lawrence*

Informal's what women always say they're going to be and never are. *Christopher Morley*

As any psychologist will tell you, the worst thing you can possibly do to a woman is deprive her of a grievance.

Beverley Nichols

Women would rather be right than reasonable.

Ogden Nash

The woman whose behaviour indicates that she will make a scene if she is told the truth asks to be deceived.

Elizabeth Jenkins

Women's work is always towards wholeness.

May Sarton

Hysteria is a natural phenomenon, the common denominator of the female nature. It's the big female weapon, and the test of a man is his ability to cope with it.

Tennessee Williams

♮

To tell a woman what she may not do is to tell her what she can.

Spanish proverb

Winter weather and women's thoughts change oft.

*

It is no more pity to see a woman weep than to see a goose go barefoot.

*

Women are saints in church, angels in the street, devils in the kitchen, and apes in bed.

*

A woman's tongue is the last thing about her that dies.

*

Women laugh when they can and weep when they will.

Anon.

37

Intuition
and the Heart

Purity of heart is the noblest inheritance, and love the fairest
ornament of women.   *Marcus Aurelius Claudius*

Earth has nothing more tender than a woman's heart when it
is the abode of piety.   *Martin Luther*

Ah, sentiments of mercy are in unison with a woman's heart.
                                                       Catherine de' Medici

How weak a thing
The heart of woman is!

William Shakespeare

The closet of a bad woman's thought is ever open, and the depth of her heart hath a string that stretcheth to her tongue.

R.M.

. . . please to remember that I have only the outside of a woman, and that my heart and mind are wholly masculine.

Ninon de Lenclos

The intuitions of women are better and readier than those of men; her quick decisions without conscious reasons, are frequently far superior to a man's most careful deductions.

William Aikman

What female heart can gold despise?
What cat's averse to fish?

Thomas Gray

A coquette is a woman without any heart, who makes a fool out of a man that hasn't got any head.

Dorothée Luzy

Women have more heart and more imagination than men.

*

God has placed the genius of women in their hearts; because the works of this genius are always works of love.

Alphonse de Lamartine

Divination seems heightened to its highest power in woman.

Bronson Alcott

Men have sight; women insight.

Victor Hugo

A woman too often reasons from her heart; hence two-thirds of her mistakes and her troubles.

Edward George Bulwer-Lytton

The surest way to hit a woman's heart is to take aim kneeling.

Douglas Jerrold

I would have a woman as true as Death. At the first real lie which works from the heart outward, she should be tenderly chloroformed into a better world.

Oliver Wendell Holmes

. . . a woman's heart must be of such a size and no larger, else it must be pressed small, like Chinese feet . . .

George Eliot

With women the heart argues, not the mind.

Matthew Arnold

Women have a wonderful instinct about things. They can discover everything except the obvious.

Oscar Wilde

Of course women's hearts beat – they beat constantly – for people who are not husbands.

Elinor Glyn

A woman's guess is much more accurate than a man's certainty.

Rudyard Kipling

The heart of a woman is never so full of affection that there does not remain a little corner for flattery and love.

Julien Mauveaux

What passes for woman's intuition is often nothing more than man's transparency.

George Jean Nathan

Women and birds are able to see without turning their heads, and that is indeed a necessary provision, for they are both surrounded by enemies.

James Stephens

All women are not Helen . . . but have Helen in their hearts.

William Carlos Williams

Women have no wilderness in them,
They are provident instead,
Content in the tight hot cell of their hearts
To eat dusty bread.

Louise Bogan

A woman without intuition is a bird without wings.

Robin Skelton

May woman's charm be dependent on neither eyes, hair nor complexion, but on heart.

*

When a woman has an affair of the heart, she goes into ecstasies; a man goes into details.

*

Man has shown good logic in encouraging feminine instincts, for they have played women stupendous tricks.

*

A woman's heart, like the moon, is always changing, but there is always a man in it.   *Anon.*

Virtue, Modesty,
Woman on a Pedestal

A virtuous woman is a crown to her husband.

Proverbs 12:4

For a silence and a chaste reserve is woman's genuine praise,
and to remain quiet within the house.

Euripides

A woman who has sacrificed her modesty can refuse nothing.

Tacitus

'Woman' must ever be a woman's highest name,
And honours more than 'Lady', if I know right.

Walther von der Vogelweide

A handsome woman is a jewel; a good woman is a treasure.

Saadi

Honour to Womankind! It needs must be that God loves Woman, since He fashioned Thee.

Christine de Pisan, of Joan of Arc

Her voice was ever soft,
Gentle and low, an excellent thing in woman.

*

'Tis beauty, that doth oft make women proud;
But, God He knows, thy share thereof is small:
'Tis virtue that doth make them most admir'd.

*

Women are the books, the arts, the academies, that show, contain, and nourish all the world.

William Shakespeare

There is something in a woman beyond all human delight; a magnetic virtue, a charming quality, an occult and powerful motive.

Robert Burton

A virtuous woman is a hidden treasure; he who has found one makes quite certain of not boasting of it.

*

There are few virtuous women who are not tired of their role.

*

Virtue in women is often only love of their reputation and of their quiet.

La Rochefoucauld

There are moments when women would rather be treated a little roughly than with too much consideration; men are more often defeated because of their own clumsiness than because of a woman's virtue.

Ninon de Lenclos

Silence is the ornament of women.

Anne Dacier

An artful woman makes a modern saint.

Matthew Prior

Men who cherish for women the highest respect are seldom popular with [them].

Joseph Addison

Woman, the last, the best reserved of God.

Alexander Pope

All the reasonings of men are not worth one sentiment of women.

Voltaire

Women commonly eat more sparingly, and are less curious in the choice of meat; but if once you find a woman gluttonous, expect from her very little virtue.

Dr Johnson

Nature intended that woman should be her masterpiece.

Gotthold Ephraim Lessing

Women are the poetry of the world in the same sense as the stars are the poetry of heaven. – Clear, light-giving, harmonious, they are the terrestrial planets that rule the destinies of mankind.

Francis Hargrave

The Eternal Feminine draws us on (or, upward).

Johann Wolfgang von Goethe

The nakedness of woman is the work of God.

William Blake

Purity of mind and conduct is the first glory of a woman.

Germaine de Staël

In most sudden accidents, and in all domestic misfortune, female resolution and presence of mind are indispensably requisite to safety, health, and life often depends upon the fortitude of women.

Maria Edgeworth

A perfect woman, nobly planned,
To warn, to comfort and command.

William Wordsworth

The foundation of domestic happiness is faith in the virtue of women.

Walter Savage Landor

I for one venerate a petticoat.

Lord Byron

... women, wherever placed, however high or low in the scale of cultivation, hold the destinies of humankind.

Frances Wright

A woman has this quality in common with the angels, that those who suffer belong to her.

Honoré de Balzac

No one knows like a woman how to say things which are at once gentle and deep.

Victor Hugo

A sufficient and sure method of civilization is the influence of good women.

Ralph Waldo Emerson

Love is the virtue of women.

George Sand

A woman's chastity consists, like an onion, of a series of coats.

Nathaniel Hawthorne

A good and true woman is said to resemble a Cremona fiddle — age but increases its worth and sweetens its tone.

Nature is in earnest when she makes a woman.

Oliver Wendell Holmes

The especial genius of women I believe to be electrical in movement, intuitive in function, spiritual in tendency.

Margaret Fuller

Contact with a high-minded woman is good for the life of any man.

Henry Vincent

If there be any one whose power is in beauty, in purity, in goodness, it is a woman.

Henry Ward Beecher

Earth's noblest thing, a woman perfected.

James Russell Lowell

Next to God we are indebted to woman, first for life itself, and then for making it worth having.

Christian Nestell Bovee

Maidens should be mild and meek,
Swift to hear and slow to speak.

Charlotte M. Yonge

God's rarest blessing is, after all, a good woman.

George Meredith

Woman embroiders man's life – Embroider is to beautify – The embroidery of cleanliness – Of a smile – Of gentle words.

Mary Wood Allen

Wicked women bother one. Good women bore one. That is the only difference between them.

*

I am on the side of the Trojans.
They fought for a woman.

*

A misanthrope I can understand – a womanthrope never.

Oscar Wilde

Many women plume themselves upon their impregnable virtue, who have never met *the* man.

Minna Antrim

O Woman, you are not merely the handiwork of God, but also of men; these are ever endowing you with beauty from their own hearts . . . You are one-half woman and one-half dream.

Sir Rabindranath Tagore

Many thoroughly good and virtuous wives and mothers feel that no nice-minded woman would want things to look becoming in bed.

Elinor Glyn

Somebody must be longsuffering and meek. With all their follies and vanities and limitations, it has been the women who have always practised this negative but essential virtue.

Corra May Harris

There is not a woman in the world the possession of whom is as precious as that of the truth which she reveals to us by causing us to suffer.

Marcel Proust

So long as the average prostitute is able to make a good living, she is quite content with her lot, and disposed to contrast it egotistically with the slavery of her virtuous sisters.

*

No woman is honestly meek.

H.L. Mencken

Woman was *too* perfect so God made the coquette.

Walter Pulitzer

The entire being of a woman is a secret which should be kept.

Isak Dinesen

A woman can look both moral and exciting – if she also looks as if it was quite a struggle.

Edna Ferber

Most good women are hidden treasures who are only safe
because nobody looks for them.
Dorothy Parker

A woman that's too soft and sweet is like tapioca pudding —
fine for them as likes it.
Osa Johnson

Woman's virtue is man's greatest invention.
Cornelia Otis Skinner

The mystery of women is largely the product of the romantic
imagination of men.
Charles Angoff

If you really worship women they'll forgive you everything,
even if your balls are dropping off.
Lawrence Durrell

Modesty makes women insincere.
Eeva-Liisa Manner

The pedestal is immobilizing and subtly insulting whether
or not some women yet realize it. We must move up from
the pedestal.
Wilma Scott Heide

There's a little bit of hooker in every woman. A little bit of
hooker and a little bit of God.
Sarah Miles

The word LADY: Most Often Used to Describe Someone You
Wouldn't Want to Talk to for Even Five Minutes.

Fran Lebowitz

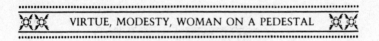
Without women the two extremes of life would be without succour, and the middle without pleasure.

Virtue, modesty and truth are the guardian angels of women.

Anon.

51

Strengths
and Weaknesses

For the lips of a strange woman drop as an honeycomb, and
her mouth is smoother than oil: But her end is bitter as
wormwood, sharp as a two-edged sword.

*

The mouth of a strange woman is a deep pit: he whom the
Lord is angry with, shall fall into it.   *Proverbs 22:14; 5:3*

There is hardly a case in which the dispute was not caused by
a woman.   *Juvenal*

Messires, I am but a poor village girl; I cannot ride on
horseback nor lead men to battle.   *Attrib. Joan of Arc*

A woman hath none other weapon but her tongue.

Thomas Becon

I know I have the body of a weak and feeble woman, but I have the heart and stomach of a king, and of a king of England too.

Queen Elizabeth I

I have often thought that the nature of women was inferior to that of man in general, but superior in particular.

Fulke Greville

To the disgrace of men it is seen, that there are women both more wise to judge what evil is expected, and more constant to bear it when it is happened.

Sir Philip Sidney

What is there in this vile earth that more commendeth a woman than constancy?

John Lyly

The venom clamors of a jealous woman
Poison more deadly than a mad dog's tooth.

*

How hard it is for women to keep counsel.

*

Make the doors upon a woman's wit, and it will out the casement; shut that, and 'twill out at the keyhole; stop that, 'twill fly with the smoke out at the chimney.

*

Frailty, thy name is woman!

William Shakespeare

If women have a will,
They'll do it 'gainst all the watches of the world.

Ben Jonson

A man can keep another person's secret better than his own: a woman, on the contrary, keeps her secret though she blabs all others.

Jean de la Bruyère

A slighted woman knows no bounds.

Sir John Vanbrugh

Who to a woman trusts his peace of mind,
Trusts a frail bark with tempestuous wind.

George Granville

Heav'n has no rage, like love to hatred turn'd,
Nor Hell a fury, like a woman scorn'd.

William Congreve

... when a Woman appears in the World under any distinguishing Character she must expect to be the mark of ill Nature.

Catherine Cockburn

Women are never stronger than when they arm themselves with their weaknesses.

Marie du Deffand

Women have a perpetual envy of our vices; they are less vicious than we, not from choice, but because we restrict them.

*

Nature has given women so much power that the law has very wisely given them little.

Dr Johnson

Women swallow at one mouthful the lie that flatters, and drink drop by drop the truth that is bitter.

*

The fault of women is that they never think of the future.

Denis Diderot

O woman! feeble and deceiving creature!

Pierre-Augustin Caron de Beaumarchais

What is a mistress? A woman in whose presence we forget what we know by heart: all the failings of her sex.

Nicolas de Chamfort

A woman is seldom roused to great and courageous exertion but when something most dear to her is in immediate danger.

*

Nay, heaven defend us from a violent woman; for that is the devil himself!

Joanna Baillie

. . . I have a woman's fears, but they cannot make me into a hypocrite or a slave.

Germaine de Staël

Most of their faults women owe to us, while we are indebted to them for most of our better qualities.

Charles Lemesle

Disguise our bondage as we will,
'Tis woman, woman, rules us still.

Thomas Moore

Woman – last at the cross, and earliest at the grave.

Eaton Stannard Barrett

Women who do not need the permanent valour of men, can always have strength from above.

Marceline Desbordes-Valmore

Woman is like the reed which bends to every breeze, but breaks not in the tempest. *Archbishop Richard Whately*

Woman, wakeful woman's never weary,
Above all, when she waits to thump her deary.

R.H. Barham

The fundamental fault of the female character is that it has no sense of justice. *Arthur Schopenhauer*

There is a woman at the beginning of all great things.

Alphonse de Lamartine

[Women] are early taught that to appear to yield, is the only way to govern. *Sarah Moore Grimké*

Nearly every folly committed by woman is born of the stupidity or evil influence of man. *Jules Michelet*

The errors of women spring, almost always, from their faith in the good, or their confidence in the true.

Honoré de Balzac

It is often woman who inspires us with the great things that she will prevent us from accomplishing.

Alexandre Dumas, père

Curiosity is one of the forms of feminine bravery.

Victor Hugo

A woman's strength is the unresistible might of weakness.

Ralph Waldo Emerson

Next to the wound, what women make best is the bandage.

Jules Barbey d'Aurevilly

There are some meannesses which are too mean even for man – woman, lovely woman alone, can venture to commit them.

*

Women like not only to conquer, but to be conquered.

William Makepeace Thackeray

Whoever embarks with women embarks with a storm; but they are themselves the safety boats.

Arsène Houssaye

When I see the elaborate study and ingenuity displayed by women in the pursuit of trifles, I feel no doubt of their capacity for the most Herculean undertakings.

Julia Ward Howe

Time and circumstance, which enlarge the views of most men, narrow the views of women almost invariably.

Thomas Hardy

A man imagines he wins by strenuous assault. The woman knows the victory was due to surrender. *Arnold Haultain*

. . . the female of the species is more deadly than the male.

*

Four things greater than all things are, —
Women and Horses and Power and War.

Rudyard Kipling

A man always mistakes a woman's clinging devotion for weakness, until he discovers that it requires the strength of Samson, the patience of Job, and the finesse of Solomon to untwine it. *Helen Rowland*

The females of all species are most dangerous when they appear to retreat. *Don Marquis*

If you let [women] have their way, you will generally get even with them in the end.

*

There is nothing as determined as a woman that carries on, and there is millions of 'em. *Will Rogers*

No genuine woman ever gives a hoot for law if law happens to stand in the way of her private interest.

*

Women not only bite in the clinches; they bite even in open fighting; they have a dental reach, so to speak, of amazing length.

*

No woman, with a free choice before her, chooses self-immolation; the most she genuinely desires in that direction is a spectacular martyrdom.

*

It takes twice as long to convert a body of women to some new fallacy as it takes to convert a body of men, and even then they halt, hesitate and are full of mordant criticisms.

H.L. Mencken

Woman must not accept; she must challenge. She must not be awed by that which has been built up around her; she must reverence that woman in her which struggles for expression.

Margaret Sanger

Treat a horse like a woman, and a woman like a horse. And they'll both win for you.

Elizabeth Arden

Ordinarily a woman is less dependable than a man because the school of life teaches her nothing of obligation.

Hildric Davenport

I hate women because they always know where things are.

James Thurber

Woman is like a teabag – you can't tell how strong she is until you put her in hot water.

Nancy Reagan

... tears ... one of the most potent weapons in woman's bitchy and inexhaustible arsenal.

Ama Ata Aidoo

Women's chief weapon is their tongue, and they will not let it rust.

French proverb

A woman's advice is a poor thing, but he is a fool who does not take it.

Spanish proverb

Women will not cease from folly as long as they live in the light of day.

*

One hair of a woman draws more than a team of oxen.

*

Women are necessary evils.

*

Women and their wills are dangerous ills.

*

Men have many faults, women only two:
There's nothing good they say, and nothing good they do.

*

Strategy in women is born of expediency.

*

A woman's strength is in her tongue.

Anon.

Friendship and
Rivalry

Woman is woman's natural ally.

*

A woman should always stand by a woman.

Euripides

... never did a woman who loved her husband succeed in loving his whore.

Catherine de' Medici

Two women placed together make cold weather.

William Shakespeare

What makes the majority of women have little feeling for friendship is that after they have tasted love it is insipid.

La Rochefoucauld

It is because of men that women dislike one another.

Jean de la Bruyère

'Tis the greatest misfortune in nature for a woman to want a confidant.

George Farquhar

To find out a girl's faults, praise her to her girl friends.

Benjamin Franklin

The endearing elegance of female friendship.

Dr Johnson

Women, like princes, find few real friends.

Lord Lyttelton

She is such a good friend that she would throw all her acquaintances into the water for the pleasure of fishing them out.

Alexandre A. Talleyrand-Périgord, of Germaine de Staël

However low an opinion a man may have of women, every woman's is worse.

Nicolas de Chamfort

The most dangerous acquaintance a married woman can make is the female confidante.

Dorothée Luzy

A man would create another man if one did not already exist, but a woman might live an eternity without even thinking of reproducing her own sex.

Johann Wolfgang von Goethe

Friendship among women is only a suspension of hostilities.

Antoine de Rivarol

... as nobody can do more mischief to a woman than a woman, so perhaps might one reverse the maxim and say nobody can do more good.

Lady Elizabeth Holland

War ... is natural to women, as well as man – at least, with their own sex!

Sydney Smith

A woman's friendship borders more closely on love than man's. Men affect each other in the reflection of noble or friendly acts; whilst women ask fewer proofs and more signs and expressions of attachment.

Samuel Taylor Coleridge

No friendship is so cordial or so delicious as that of girl for girl; no hatred so intense and immovable as that of woman for woman.

Walter Savage Landor

There is nothing which more disunites two women than to be obliged to make their devotions at the same altar.

Honoré de Balzac

Almost every woman described to you by a woman presents a tragic idea, and not an idea of well-being.

Ralph Waldo Emerson

I think there is nothing more lovely than the love of two beautiful women who are not envious of each other's charms.

*

Female friendships are of rapid growth.

Benjamin Disraeli

       The woman is so hard
Upon the woman.

Alfred, Lord Tennyson

The thing needed . . . to raise women (and to raise men too)
is these friendships without love between men and women.
And if between married men and married women, all the
better.

Florence Nightingale

A woman may very well form a friendship with a man, but
for this to endure, it must be assisted by a little physical
antipathy.

Friedrich Nietzsche

All women are rivals.

Arnold Haultain

Once a woman loses her position for a man she will lose the
man as well.

Elinor Glyn

Never praise a sister to a sister, in the hope of your
compliments reaching the proper ears.

Rudyard Kipling

Most women have all other women as their adversaries;
most men have all other men as their allies.

Gelett Burgess

When women kiss it always reminds one of prizefighters
shaking hands.

*

On one issue at least, men and women agree; they both distrust women.

H.L. Mencken

Women were cats, all of them, unless they were fools, and there was no way of getting even with them ever, except by walking off with the men they wanted.

Frances Parkinson Keyes

A woman wins men because of her beauty; women, in spite of it.

*

The response a beautiful woman receives from her sex — envy, hatred, malice, and all uncharitableness.

Hildric Davenport

Women see through each other, but they rarely look into themselves.

Theodor Reik

Intimacies between women often go backwards, beginning in revelations and ending up in small talk without loss of esteem.

Elizabeth Bowen

In mixed company, women practise a sort of visual short-hand, which, later, they will laboriously and at great length decode in the company of other women.

Malcolm de Chazal

Between women love is contemplative . . . There is no struggle, no victory, no defeat; in exact reciprocity each is at once subject and object, sovereign and slave; duality becomes mutuality.

Simone de Beauvoir

Love between women is seen as a paradigm of love between equals, and that is perhaps its greatest attraction.

Elizabeth Janeway

A witch and a bitch always dress up for each other, because otherwise the witch would upstage the bitch, or the bitch would upstage the witch, and the result would be havoc.

Tennessee Williams

No woman calls another a whore without envy.

Robin Skelton

Where they are all women there is never any lack of quarrelling.

Spanish proverb

One cannot depend on woman's friendship for she gives everything to love.

Anon.

....

Reputation and
Discretion

As a jewel of gold in a swine's snout, so is a fair woman who is without discretion.

Proverbs 11:22

A woman's greatest glory is to be little talked about by men, whether for good or ill.

Pericles

The reputation of a woman may also be compared to a mirror of crystal, shining and bright, but liable to be sullied by every breath that comes near it.

*

There are but two things that chiefly excite us to love a woman, an attractive beauty, and unspotted fame.

Miguel de Cervantes

A woman's first intrigue is not usually taken note of until she has had a second.

La Rochefoucauld

A woman with eyes only for one person, or with eyes always averted from him, creates exactly the same impression.

Jean de la Bruyère

The Natural tenderness and Delicacy of our Constitution, added to the many Dangers we are subject to from your Sex, renders it almost impossible for a Single Lady to travel without injury to her character.

Abigail Adams

It is a melancholy truth – yet such is the blessed effect of civilization! – the most respectable women are the most repressed.

Mary Wollstonecraft

The entire social order . . . is arrayed against a woman who wants to rise to a man's reputation.

Germaine de Staël

By permitting your reflection to carry you from your society, you expose yourself to very hazardous conjectures.

Lucy Hay, Countess of Carlisle

INDISCRETION: The guilt of women.

Ambrose Bierce

I reject the monstrous theory that while a man may redeem the past a woman never can.

Hall Caine

One should never trust a woman who tells her real age. A woman who would tell one that would tell one anything.

Oscar Wilde

No man can understand why a woman should prefer a good reputation to a good time.

Helen Rowland

He had fancied that a woman can shed her past like a man.

Edith Wharton

Whenever a woman goes into trade she quickly gets a reputation as a sharp trader.

H.L. Mencken

Did it ever occur to you that there's something almost crooked in the way decent girls nowadays use the shelter of their established respectability to make things awkward for men?

Margaret Culkin Banning

It's the good girls who keep diaries; the bad girls never have the time.

Tallulah Bankhead

Discreet women have neither eyes nor ears.

*

A woman's past is either scandalously indecent or shamefully uninteresting.

*

Women are seldom reluctant about giving themselves to men who consider their act a folly.

Anon.

69

***

Sex
and the Sexes

Woman once made equal to man becomes his superior.

Socrates

Woman may be said to be an inferior man.

Aristotle

A woman is necessarily an evil, and he is a lucky man who catches her in the mildest form.

Menander

Women have many faults, but the worst of them all is that they are too pleased with themselves and take too little pains to please the men.

Plautus

70

If she is pleasing to one man, a girl is taken care of.

Propertius

I hate a woman who offers herself because she ought to do so, and, cold and dry, thinks of her sewing when she's making love.

Ovid

But a woman of good character, sensible as well as virtuous, if she finds a man to her liking, oughtn't to treat him too disdainfully.

Marie de France

... the ambition of women is so great, that they never content themselves with one lover. I have heard that the best of them like to have three – one for honour, one for interest, and the third for pleasure ...

Margaret of Navarre

What man has assurance enough to pretend to know thoroughly the riddle of a woman's mind, and who could ever hope to fix her mutable nature?

Miguel de Cervantes

Would it not grieve a woman to be over-master'd with a piece of valiant dust? to make an account of her life to a clod of wayward marl?

*

Men's vows are women's traitors.

*

Were kisses all the joy in bed, one woman would another wed.

William Shakespeare

Were there no women, men might live like gods.

Thomas Dekker

Say, are not women truly, then,
Styl'd but the shadows of us men?

Ben Jonson

Of women's unnatural, unsatiable lust, what country, what village doth not complain?

*

... as matter seeks form, so does woman man.

*

Many women dote upon a man for his compliment only and good behaviour.

Robert Burton

There cannot be a greater clog to man than to be troubled with a wanton woman.

R.M.

There is no other purgatory but a woman.

Beaumont and Fletcher

... forbeare to charge women with the faults which come from the contagion of Masculine serpents.

Ester Sowernam

Words are women, deeds are men.

George Herbert

Women were created for the comfort of men.

James Howell

If thou wouldst please the ladies, thou must endeavour to make them pleased with themselves.

Thomas Fuller

72

The cruellest revenge of a woman is often to remain faithful to a man.

Jacques-Bénigne Bossuet

A woman is easily governed, if a man takes her in hand.

Jean de la Bruyère

Womankind more joy discovers
Making fools than keeping lovers.

John Wilmot, Earl of Rochester

If woman were humbler, men would be honester.

Sir John Vanbrugh

No woman can be a beauty without a fortune.

*

Women are like pictures: of no value in the hands of a fool till he hears men of sense bid high for the purchase.

George Farquhar

A shameless woman is the worst of men.

Edward Young

He that tastes woman, ruin meets.

*

'Tis woman that seduces all mankind,
By her we first were taught the wheedling arts.

John Gay

Women are not formed for great cares themselves, but to soothe and soften ours.

Lord Chesterfield

God created woman only to tame man.

Voltaire

The proof of gold is fire; the proof of a woman, gold; the proof of a man, a woman.

Benjamin Franklin

Most men like in women what is most opposite their own characters.

Henry Fielding

Woman, I tell you, is a microcosm; and rightly to rule her, requires as great talents as to govern a state.

Samuel Foote

Let men say whate'er they will,
Woman, woman, rules them still.

Isaac Bickerstaffe

There are girls who manage to sell themselves, whom none would take as gifts.

*

There are two things that I have always loved madly: they are women and celibacy.

*

Women wage with men a war in which the latter have an immense advantage, in that the loose women are all on their side.

*

You may be as charming and honourable as can be, and may love the most perfect woman imaginable; you will still find that you have to overlook your predecessor, or your successor.

*

In order for a relation between a man and a woman to amount to anything, they must share pleasure, memory or desire.

*

The passion of women forces the most honest of men to be either a husband or a gallant, either a rake or impotent.

Nicolas de Chamfort

Nature made us [women] equal to them, and gave us the power to render ourselves superior.

Susanna Haswell Rowson

As for the women, though we scorn and flout 'em,
We may live with, but cannot live without 'em.

Frederic Reynolds

The man that lays his hand upon a woman,
Save in the way of kindness, is a wretch
Whom't were gross flattery to name a coward.

John Tobin

The man's desire is for the woman; but the woman's desire is rarely other than for the desire of the man.

Samuel Taylor Coleridge

A wise woman never yields by appointment. It should always be an unforeseen happiness.

Stendhal

That which causes the tragic end of a woman's life, is often but a moment of amusement and folly in the history of a man.

*

Women, like toys, are sought after, and trifled with, and then thrown by with every varying caprice. *Lady Caroline Lamb*

I do think better of womankind than to suppose they care whether Mister John Keats five feet high likes them or not.

John Keats

The duration of passion is proportionate with the original resistance of the woman. *Honoré de Balzac*

A wretched woman is more unfortunate than a wretched man.

*

Men are women's playthings; woman is the devil's.

Victor Hugo

A woman is more responsive to a man's forgetfulness than to his attentions. *Jules Janin*

We censure the inconstancy of women when we are the victims; we find it charming when we are the objects.

Louis Desnoyers

If men knew all that women think, they would be twenty times more audacious. *Alphonse Karr*

In Paris, when God provides a beautiful woman, the devil at once retorts with a fool to keep her. *Jules Barbey d'Aurevilly*

A woman never forgets her sex. She would rather talk with a man than an angel, any day.

*

Man has his will — but woman has her way.

Oliver Wendell Holmes

When the man wants weight, the woman takes it up,
And topples down the scales.

*

Woman is not undevelopt man,
But diverse.

*

Man is the hunter; woman is his game.

*

God made the woman for the man.

Alfred, Lord Tennyson

The costliest women are the ones who cost nothing.

Alfred de Musset

'Tis strange what a man may do, and a woman yet think him an angel. *William Makepeace Thackeray*

Woman's degradation is in man's idea of his sexual rights.

Elizabeth Cady Stanton

I'm not denyin' the women are foolish: God Almighty made 'em to match the men.

*

It is a common enough case, that of a man being suddenly captivated by a woman nearly the opposite of his ideal.

*

I should like to know what is the proper function of women, if it is not to make reasons for husbands to stay at home, and still stronger reasons for bachelors to go out. *George Eliot*

[Woman] is at once the delight and the terror of man.

Henri-Frédéric Amiel

There are many different types of men, there is only one woman.

Edmond de Goncourt

Men who do not make advances to women are apt to become victims to women who make advances to them.

Walter Bagehot

The best woman has always somewhat of a man's strength; and the noblest man of a woman's gentleness.

*

The deepest tenderness a woman can show to a man, is to help him do his duty.

Mrs Craik

I expect that Woman will be the last thing civilised by Man.

George Meredith

I heard a man say that brigands demand your money or your life, whereas women require both. *Attrib. Samuel Butler*

Woman would be more charming if one could fall into her arms without falling into her hands.

Ambrose Bierce

For a man to pretend to understand women is bad manners; for him to really understand them is bad morals.

Henry James

I think every woman, in her heart of hearts, *wishes* to be ravished; but naturally it must be by the right man.

Edward Carpenter

There are two things a real man likes — danger and play; and he likes woman because she is the most dangerous of playthings.

Friedrich Nietzsche

I am a source of satisfaction to him, a nurse, a piece of furniture, a *woman* — nothing more.

Sophie Tolstoy

What attracts us in a woman rarely binds us to her.

John Churton Collins

It is the law of eternal justice that man cannot degrade women without himself falling into degradation; and he cannot raise them without himself becoming better.

A. Martien

It is delightful to be a woman; but every man thanks the Lord devoutly that he isn't one.

Olive Schreiner

Women give to men the very gold of their lives . . . but they invariably want it back in such very small change.

*

The Book of Life begins with a man and a woman in a garden.
It ends with Revelations.

*

All women become like their mothers. That is their tragedy.
No man does. That is his.

*

Women represent the triumph of matter over mind, just as
men represent the triumph of mind over morals.

Oscar Wilde

The only way for a woman to provide for herself decently is
for her to be good to some man that can afford to be good to
her.

George Bernard Shaw

... women know men better than they know themselves
and better than men ever suspect ...

Sir John Willison

Being a woman is a terribly difficult task, since it consists
principally in dealing with men.

Joseph Conrad

Most men who rail against women are railing at one woman
only.

Remy de Gourmont

... it is not true that woman was made from man's rib; she
was made from his funny bone.

Sir J.M. Barrie

... with her overcharged sensibility, her prominent
modesty, her 'eternal femininity' – the female genus homo
is undeniably over-sexed.

Charlotte Perkins Gilman

To control a man a woman must first control herself.

*

Man is kind only to be cruel; women cruel only to be kind.

*

Man forgives woman anything save the wit to outwit him.

Minna Antrim

Women have changed in their relationship to men, but men stand pat just where Adam did when it comes to dealing with women.

Dorothy Dix

Men are like the earth and we are like the moon; we turn always one side to them and they think there is no other.

Olive Schreiner

Men continually study women, and know nothing about them. Women never study men, and know all about them.

*

If a man understands one woman he should let it go at that.

Bob Edwards

If a woman absolutely worships a man – even if she is only his mother – she is bound to find many moments of unhappiness.

*

It is difficult for a dowdy, faithful woman to keep the devotion of a man, however good and dear she may be. These qualities do not suit male creatures as well as caprice, it seems.

*

It would take some men five years to degrade themselves sufficiently to be able to enjoy the society of modern women.

*

The 'place' of a man is doing exactly what the particular woman in the case wants him to do.

Elinor Glyn

Take my word for it, the silliest woman can manage a clever man; but it needs a very clever woman to manage a fool.

Rudyard Kipling

Nothing ages a man like living always with the same woman.

Norman Douglas

Women have taken over half a man's world, and kept the whole of their own.

Stephen Leacock

An absence, the decline of a dinner invitation, an unintentional coldness, can accomplish more than all the cosmetics and beautiful dresses in the world.

Marcel Proust

[To men] all women are monkeys. They're interested only in our absurdities and our love affairs and our illnesses.

*

He wondered why sexual shyness, which excites the desire of dissolute women, arouses the contempt of decent ones.

Colette

Men are men, but Man is a woman.

*

The two things that a healthy person hates most between heaven and hell are a woman who is not dignified and a man who is.

G.K. Chesterton

A woman occasionally is quite a serviceable substitute for masturbation. It takes an abundance of imagination to be sure.
Karl Kraus

The same woman may be a goddess to a boy, a temptation to a married man, and a 'menace' to a bachelor.

*

It takes a woman twenty years to make a man of her son, and another woman twenty minutes to make a fool of him.

*

Failing to be there when a man wants her is woman's greatest sin, except to be there when he doesn't want her.
Helen Rowland

There is no book on woman by a man that is not a stupendous compendium of posturings and imbecilities.

*

It is almost impossible to find a man who honestly wishes that he were a woman, but almost every woman, at some time or another in her life, is gnawed by a regret that she is not a man.

*

Nine men out of ten would be quite happy, I believe, if there were no women in the world, once they had grown accustomed to the quiet.

*

There are, of course, women who spend a great deal of time denouncing and reviling men, but these are certainly not genuine man-haters; they are simply women who have done their best to snare men, and failed.

*

If it were advertised that a troupe of men of easy virtue were to appear half-clothed upon a public stage, exposing their chests, thighs, arms and calves, the only women who would go to the entertainment would be a few delayed adolescents, a psychopathic old maid or two, and a guard of indignant members of the parish Ladies' Aid Society.

H.L Mencken

The way to fight a woman is with your hat. Grab it and run.

John Barrymore

The residue of virility in the woman's [sexual] organism is utilized by nature in order to eroticize her: otherwise the functioning of the maternal apparatus would wholly submerge her in the painful tasks of reproduction and motherhood.

Marie Bonaparte

To win a woman in the first place one must please her, then undress her, and then somehow get her clothes back on her. Finally, so she will allow you to leave her, you've got to annoy her.

Jean Giraudoux

Something depressing comes on the mind when it has been too excessively occupied with the female sex.

James Stephens

Women have served all these centuries as looking glasses possessing the . . . power of reflecting the figure of man at twice its size.

Virginia Woolf

The best man for a man and the best man for a woman are not the same.

José Ortega y Gasset

84

A woman does not relinquish one man until she secures another.

*

Women's Fates: – *Men*.
Women's Misfortunes: – *Other Men*.

*

The woman who believes her lover to be unlike other men, understands neither the man nor the sex.

*

Women must always pretend not to be willing – men must always pretend not to be aware of the fact.

*

Woman idealizes love, man idealizes woman.

Hildric Davenport

The art of being a woman can never consist of being a bad imitation of a man.

Olga Knopf

When a man makes her laugh, a woman feels protected.

Ugo Betti

When women go wrong, men go right after them.

Mae West

Woman wants monogamy;
Man delights in novelty.

Dorothy Parker

Behind every successful man there is a surprised woman.

Attrib. Maryon Pearson

Women are quite unlike men. Women have higher voices, longer hair, smaller waistlines, daintier feet and prettier hands. They also invariably have the upper hand.

Stephen Potter

Most women set out to try to change a man, and when they have changed him they do not like him.

Attrib. Marlene Dietrich

The average man is more interested in a woman who is interested in him than he is in a woman – any woman – with beautiful legs.

Marlene Dietrich

Women want mediocre men, and men are working to be as mediocre as possible.

Margaret Mead

Woman is not an equal but rather a sequel to man.

Dagobert D. Runes

Women are a dime a dozen . . . but it's when you cut the number down to one that it starts costing.

John Steinbeck

A woman who will not feign submission can never make a man happy.

*

In the sex-war, thoughtlessness is the weapon of the male, vindictiveness of the female.

Cyril Connolly

There's no human being a man can buy anymore – except a woman.

Clare Boothe Luce

I am a woman meant for a man, but I never found a man who could compete.

Bette Davis

Woman gives herself as a prize to the weak and as a prop to the strong, and no man ever has what he should.

Cesare Pavese

To the mind of the modern girl, legs, like busts, are power points which she has been taught to tailor, but as parts of the success kit rather than erotically or sensuously.

Marshall McLuhan

The sex symbol always remains, but the sophisticated woman has become old hat.

Rosalind Russell

There are women who offer their bodies as though they were bestowing some inestimable gift upon you.

John Hearn

Behind almost every woman you ever heard of stands a man who let her down.

Naomi Bliven

The problem is to make the woman know that she wants you.

Roger Vadim

According to recent studies, those men who don't understand women fall into two groups: bachelors and husbands.

Jacques Languirand

It is possible that blondes also prefer gentlemen.

Mamie Van Doren

A woman without a man is like a fish without a bicycle.

Gloria Steinem

There aren't any hard women, only soft men.

Raquel Welch

Men play the game; women know the score.

Roger Woddis

All women are trollops.

French proverb

Woman is the woe of man.

Latin proverb

There are more secret whores than open ones.

Russian proverb

He who is ignored by women is most fortunate.

Spanish proverb

A woman, a dog, and a walnut tree,
The more you beat them, the better they'll be.

*

A man of straw is worth a woman of gold.

*

Women are entitled to life, liberty, and the pursuit of man.

*

After man came woman — and she has been after him ever since.

*

After a man finds out that the woman is no angel, he tries to ascertain to what extent she isn't.

*

In courtship a man pursues a woman until she catches him.

*

For every woman who makes a fool out of a man there is another woman who makes a man out of a fool.

Anon.

Love
and Marriage

What else goes wrong for a woman — except her marriage?

*

Man's best possession is a sympathetic wife.

Euripides

But what a woman says to her desirous lover should be written in wind and swift-flowing water. *Catullus*

Women, deceived by men, want to marry them; it is a kind of revenge as good as any other. *Philippe de Remi Beaumanoir*

To me it seems much better to love a woman as a woman, than to make her one's idol, as many do.

Margaret of Navarre

Demonstrations of love are never altogether displeasing to women, and the most disdainful, in spite of all their coyness, reserve a little complaisance in their hearts for their admirers.

Miguel de Cervantes

Wives are young men's mistresses, companions for middle age, and old men's nurses.

Francis Bacon

. . . maids are May when they are maids, but the sky changes when they are wives.

*

Maids want nothing but husbands, and
When they have them, they want everything.

*

Hanging and wiving go by destiny.

*

War is no strife
To the dark house and the detested wife.

Shakespeare

Of all the paths lead to a woman's love,
Pity's the straightest.

Beaumont and Fletcher

Women love out of fancy,
Men from advice.

Shackerley Marmion

In their first passions women love the lover, and in the others they are in love with love.

*

A woman often thinks she regrets the lover, when she only regrets the love.

*

Of all violent passions, love is the least unbecoming to women.

*

You can find women who have never had a love affair; but it is rare to find any who have had only one.

*

Women in love forgive great indiscretions more easily than little infidelities.

La Rochefoucauld

And love ties a woman's mind
    Looser than with ropes of hay.

Andrew Marvell

A husband is a plaster that cures all the ills of girlhood.

Molière

Nuns and married women are equally unhappy, if in different ways.

Queen Christina of Sweden

A Wife is to thank God her Husband hath faults ... A Husband without faults is a dangerous Observer.

*

Next to the danger of committing the Fault yourself, the greatest is that of seeing it in your Husband.

Lord Halifax

Women exceed the generality of men in love.

*

When a woman no longer loves a man, she forgets the very favours she has granted him.

Jean de la Bruyère

And if a Woman can neither Love nor Honour she does ill in promising to Obey, since she is like to have a crooked Rule to regulate her Actions.

Mary Astell

The reason why so few marriages are happy, is, because young ladies spend their time in making nets, not in making cages.

Jonathan Swift

A woman seldom asks advice before she has bought her wedding clothes.

*

Women who have been happy in a first marriage, are most apt to venture upon a second.

Joseph Addison

Her tears, her vows are all a cheat,
For woman loves herself alone.

William Somerville

How a little love and good company improves a woman!

George Farquhar

No woman would ever marry if she had not the chance of mortality for a release.

John Gay

A man loved by a beautiful woman will always get out of trouble.

Voltaire

A man will sometimes rage at his wife, when in reality his mistress has offended him; and a lady complain of the cruelty of her husband, when she has no other enemy than bad cards.

*

A good wife is like the ivy which beautifies the building to which it clings, twining its tendrils more lovingly as time converts the ancient edifice into a ruin.

Dr Johnson

One could name a woman who has made herself wretched for life and braved loss and dishonour for a lover whom she subsequently ceased to love because he removed his powder or trimmed a fingernail badly, or put on his stocking wrong side out.

Nicolas de Chamfort

Love lessens woman's delicacy and increases man's.

*

To rescue, to revenge, to instruct or protect a woman is all the same as to love her.

Jean Paul Richter

Love, which is only an episode in the life of a man, is the entire history of a woman's life.

Germaine de Staël

Men marry to make an end; women to make a beginning.

Alexis Dupuy

It is always incomprehensible to a man that a woman should refuse an offer of marriage.

*

An engaged woman is always more agreeable than a disengaged. She is satisfied with herself. Her cares are over, and she feels that she may exert all her powers of pleasing without suspicion.

Jane Austen

Even if women were immortal, they could never foresee their last lover.

Félicité-Robert de Lamennais

Man's love is of man's life a thing apart,
  'Tis woman's whole existence.

*

Though women are angels, yet wedlock's the devil.

Lord Byron

Marriage with a good woman is a harbour in the tempest of life; with a bad woman, it is a tempest in the harbour.

Jean-Antoine Petite-Senn

Losing her faith in the moral worth of the man she loves, a woman loses all the *happiness* of love.

Thérèse Albertine Louise Robinson

Marriage . . . is still the imperfect institution it must remain while women continue to be ill-educated, passive, and subservient . . .

Harriet Martineau

A woman whom we truly love is a religion.

Émile de Girardin

I have always thought that every woman should marry, and no man.

Benjamin Disraeli

Where love is absent there can be no woman.

George Sand

... thou art blind to the danger of marrying a woman who feels and acts out of the principle of equal rights ...

Angelina Grimké

If a man really loves a woman, of course he wouldn't marry her for the world if he were not quite sure that he was the best person she could by any possibility marry.

Oliver Wendell Holmes

Our hour of love will teach a woman more of her true relations than all your philosophizing.

Margaret Fuller

This I set down as a positive truth. A woman with fair opportunities and without an absolute hump, may marry whom she likes.

William Makepeace Thackeray

> All women love great men
If young or old.

Robert Browning

Woman's love is writ in water, woman's faith is traced in sand.

William E. Aytoun

The most precious possession that ever comes to a man in this world is a woman's heart.

*

A woman in love is a very poor judge of character.

J.G. Holland

[Woman's] lot is made for her by the love she accepts.

A woman dictates before marriage, in order that she may have an appetite for submission afterwards. *George Eliot*

A woman despises a man for loving her, unless she happens to return his love. *Elizabeth Stoddard*

Men love at first, and most warmly; women love last and longest. *George William Curtis*

Would you hurt a woman worst, aim at her affections.

Lew Wallace

I had rather live with the woman I love in a world full of trouble, than to live in heaven with nobody but men.

Robert G. Ingersoll

What is it that love does to a woman? Without it she only sleeps; with it, alone she lives. *Ouida*

Woman's vanity demands that a man be more than a happy husband. *Friedrich Nietzsche*

In women pity begets love, in men love begets pity.

John Churton Collins

Lastly (and this is, perhaps, the golden rule), no woman should marry a teetotaller, or a man who does not smoke.

Robert Louis Stevenson

A man who marries a woman to educate her falls into the same fallacy as the woman who marries a man to reform him.

Elbert Hubbard

When a woman marries again it is because she detested her first husband. When a man marries again it is because he adored his first wife. Women try their luck; men risk theirs.

*

The amount of women in London who flirt with their own husbands is perfectly scandalous. It looks so bad. It is simply washing one's clean linen in public.

*

Forty years of romance make a woman look like a ruin and forty years of marriage make her look like a public building.

*

Men always want to be a woman's first love, women like to be a man's last romance.

*

Men marry because they are tired; women because they are curious. Both are disappointed.

Oscar Wilde

Female murderers get sheaves of offers of marriage.

*

It is a woman's business to get married as soon as possible, and a man's to keep unmarried as long as he can.

George Bernard Shaw

Marriage is the woman's proper sphere, her divinely ordered place, her natural end. It is what she is born for, what she is trained for, what she is exhibited for. It is, moreover, her means of honorable livelihood and advancement. *But* she must not even look as if she wanted it!

Charlotte Perkins Gilman

If men knew how women pass the time when they are alone, they'd never marry.

O. Henry

If women are rarely seen and ordinarily not spoken to; if all imagination has to build upon is a furtive glance or casual motion, people fall in love at first sight.

George Santayana

Marriage is the aim and end of all sensible girls, because it is the meaning of life.

Elinor Glyn

A woman is never too old to be touched by the faithfulness of an old lover.

Evelyn Schuyler Schaeffer

As the cat lapses into savagery by night, and barbarously explores the dark, so primal and titanic is a woman with the love-madness.

Gelett Burgess

How love for a man not her husband will sharpen a woman's wits!

Norman Douglas

My idea of walking into the jaws of death is to marry some woman who has lost three husbands.

Kin Hubbard

An ideal wife is any woman who has an ideal husband.

Booth Tarkington

A woman we love rarely satisfies all our needs, and we deceive her with a woman whom we do not love.

Marcel Proust

. . . the total amount of undesired sex endured by women is probably greater in marriage than in prostitution.

Bertrand Russell

The woman is increasingly aware that love alone can give her full stature, just as the man begins to discern that spirit alone can endow his life with its highest meaning.

Carl Jung

Nothing annoys a man as to hear a woman promising to love him 'forever' when he merely wanted her to love him for a few weeks.

Helen Rowland

I married beneath me. All women do.

Nancy Astor

To be the wife of an ordinary man, indeed, is an experience that must be very hard to bear.

*

Let a woman have a husband whose conduct is not reasonably open to question, and she will invent mythical offences to make him bearable.

*

A woman, if she hates her husband (and many of them do), can make life so sour and obnoxious to him that even death on the gallows seems sweet by comparison.

*

The weight of opinion among women is decidedly against the woman who falls in love with an Apollo. She is regarded, at best, as a flighty creature, and at worst, as one pushing bad taste to the point of indecency.

*

Love is the delusion that one woman differs from another.

H.L. Mencken

A woman takes care not to show her claws until a man has shown his love.

Walter Pulitzer

Love is the delightful interval between meeting a beautiful girl and discovering that she looks like a haddock.

John Barrymore

Modern woman cannot get away from love. She is no new woman.

Benito Mussolini

Alas! For all the pretty women who marry dull men,
Go into the suburbs and never come out again.

Anna Wickham

When a man steals your wife, there is no better revenge than to let him keep her.

Sacha Guitry

How much more appreciative they would be if husbands were only wives for a while!

*

Women love — men make love.

*

A man marries a domestic woman — and is pained by her social limitations. He bestows himself upon a coquette — and is distressed by her flirtatious propensities. He takes to himself a blue-stocking — and is saddened by her inability to cook. Pre-nuptial attractions are post-nuptial distractions.

Hildric Davenport

With all her experience, every woman expects to do better when she marries a second time, and some do.

William Feather

An archaeologist is the best husband any woman can have — the older she gets the more interested he is in her.

Agatha Christie

I think every woman's entitled to a middle husband she can forget.

Adela Rogers St Johns

A wife has a lot of nerve expecting her husband to be faithful when she gets old and fat.

*

Women have two rackets going for them — marriage and alimony.

Groucho Marx

There are two great moments in a woman's life: when first she finds herself to be deeply in love with her man, and when she leaves him.

*

There is no fury like a woman searching for a new lover.

Cyril Connolly

Love makes *intelligent* beings depressed and flat. Only women, ostriches and monkeys are made happy by love. Oh yes, and parrots.

Eeva-Liisa Manner

A girl must marry for love, and keep on marrying until she finds it.

Zsa Zsa Gabor

Women embark on marriage, while men drop anchor.

Robin Skelton

Marriage: love gone – woman stays.

Robert Zend

You can either love women or know them; there's no middle way.

French proverb

Wives and water-melons are picked by chance.

Greek proverb

Women love most, by whom they are most tried.

*

He that doth not love a woman sucked a sow.

*

Women wish to marry their first love; men do not marry even their last.

*

A good wife makes a good husband.

*

When a woman marries her equal she condescends.

*

Women make marriage enduring; they do not seem to weary of its commonplace.

*

A woman who loves does not fear ridicule; a man in love knows no pride.

*

A woman who pretends to laugh at love is like a child who sings at night when he is afraid.

*

In a woman in love, the hope of discovery is an intoxication; caution exists only in the woman who is indifferent.

*

Woman spoils her first lover and practically ruins all the rest.

Anon.

Motherhood, Family, and the Home

If women did not exist, and children could be produced without them, mankind would be rid of its troubles.

*

Families can ill spare a man [by death]; women are not such a loss.

Euripides

For like as women take a greater pride in their beauty than pleasure or content in their virtue, so they take more pride in being with child than in having a child.

*

Many times married women desire children, as maids do husbands, more for honour than for comfort or happiness, thinking it a disgrace to live old maids, and so likewise to be barren.

Margaret Cavendish

Women, then, are only children of a larger growth.

Lord Chesterfield

O what's a table richly spread
Without a woman at its head!

Thomas Wharton

It would seem that women's brains had one compartment less and their hearts one string more than men's. They needed some special ordering to enable them to support, care for and cherish children.

Nicolas de Chamfort

The future of society is in the hands of mothers; if the world was lost through woman she alone can save it.

Louis de Beaufort

Meek wives are, in general, foolish mothers; wanting their children to love them best, and take their part, in secret, against the father, who is held up as a scarecrow.

*

... whatever tends to incapacitate the maternal character, takes woman out of her sphere.

Mary Wollstonecraft

With women all ideas easily become human beings.

Jean Paul Richter

Is not a small house best? Put a woman into a small house, and after five years she comes out large and healthy.

Ralph Waldo Emerson

Maids must be wives and mothers to fulfil the entire and holiest end of woman's being.

Fanny Kemble

Womanliness means only motherhood:
All love begins and ends there, – roams enough,
But, having run the circle, rests at home.

Robert Browning

The mother's heart is the child's schoolroom.

Henry Ward Beecher

... the woman is uniformly sacrificed to the wife and mother.

Elizabeth Cady Stanton

The hand that rocks the cradle
Is the hand that rules the world.

William Ross Wallace

Those of you who have the talent to do honor to poor womanhood, have all given yourself over to baby-making ...

Susan B. Anthony

Woman is the salvation or destruction of the family. She carries its destinies in the folds of her mantle.

Henri-Frédéric Amiel

Women, who are, beyond all doubt, the mothers of all mischief, also nurse that babe to sleep when he is too noisy.

R.D. Blackmore

Mother-love . . . hath this unlikeness to any other love: tender to the object, it can be infinitely tyrannical to itself, and thence all its power of self-sacrifice.
Lew Wallace

Motherhood is, after all, woman's great and incomparable work.
Edward Carpenter

Women are skeery, unless they have a home.
Will Carleton

Motherhood has . . . for many women ceased to be the sweet secret dream of the maiden, the glad hope of the wife, the deep regret of the ageing woman who has not had this yearning satisfied.
Ellen Key

Home is the girl's prison and the woman's workhouse.
George Bernard Shaw

To the old saying that man built the house but woman made of it a 'home' might be added the modern supplement that woman accepted cooking as a chore but man has made of it a recreation.
Emily Post

The rigid limitation of offspring, in fact, is chiefly advocated by women who run no more risk of having unwilling motherhood forced upon them than so many mummies of the Tenth Dynasty.
H.L. Mencken

Too many homes are built on foundations of crushed women.
Sir Clough Williams-Ellis

It is commanded that she forgive her enemies, but it is too much to expect a woman to forgive her in-laws.

Hildric Davenport

Woman's work! Housework's the hardest work in the world. That's why men won't do it.
Edna Ferber

There is nothing enduring in the life of a woman except what she builds in a man's heart.
Dame Judith Anderson

Some women are buried in coffins, but the majority are buried in bungalows.
Richard J. Needham

One sometimes has the impression that American women have a kind of dish-washing fixation.
Françoise Giroud

Being a mother is a noble status, right? Right. So why does it change when you put 'unwed' or 'welfare' in front of it?

Florynce R. Kennedy

Women! There isn't anything so bad that they don't soon start to enjoy it. Even if they lived in a barrel of shit they'd start making a home out of it, with everything nice and cozy.

Eeva-Liisa Manner

Women use children as excuses not to do anything.

Shirley Ann Grau

It is the woman who is ultimately held responsible for pregnancy. While not being allowed to have control over her body, she is nevertheless held responsible for its products.

Carol Glassman

The best thing that could happen to motherhood already has. Fewer women are going into it.

Victoria Billings

The house goes mad when women gad.

Anon.

Career

If women are expected to do the same work as men, we must teach them the same things.

Plato

I, a woman, have dropped the symbols of my sex,
Yarn, shuttle, basket, thread.

Olimpia Morata

An honest woman and a broken leg are best at home, and for an honest girl a job of work's her holiday.

Miguel de Cervantes

To man belong professions, dignities, authorities, and pleasures; for women, there remain only duties, domestic virtue, and perhaps as a result of these, the happiness of tranquil submission.

Sarah Wentworth Morton

It is certainly true that housekeeping cares bring with them a thousand endearing compensations. They are a woman's peculiar joy, and women are apt to be light-hearted.

Marceline Desbordes-Valmore

... it is only in the eyes of the vulgar-minded and the foolish, that a woman is degraded by exerting her ingenuity or her talents as a means of support. *Eliza Leslie*

... it is important that young females should possess some employment by which they might obtain a livelihood in case they should be reduced to the necessity of supporting themselves. *Lydia Howard Sigourney*

In most families, it is considered a matter of far more consequence to call a girl off from making a pie, or a pudding, than to interrupt her whilst engaged in her studies.

Sarah Moore Grimké

No amount of preaching, exhortation, sympathy, benevolence, will render the condition of our working women what it should be so long as the kitchen and the needle are substantially their only resources. *Horace Greeley*

Modern invention has banished the spinning wheel, and the same law of progress makes the woman of today a different woman from her grandmother. *Susan B. Anthony*

The women who do the most work get the least money, and the women who have the most money do the least work.

Charlotte Perkins Gilman

As to the great mass of working girls and women, how much independence is gained if the narrowness and lack of freedom of the home is exchanged for the narrowness and lack of freedom of the factory, sweatshop, department store, or office?

Emma Goldman

The greatest weakness of women [who seek careers] is that they have never been trained to work like men. I mean trained so from infancy. Men are brought up in the tradition that men must work.

John B. Watson

But, oh, what a woman I would be if an able young man would consecrate his life to me as secretaries and technicians do to their men employers.

Mabel Ulrich

The modern woman is a social problem. She is intelligent, accomplished, brilliant — better equipped for a career than for matrimony.

Hildric Davenport

It is clearly absurd that it should be possible for a woman to qualify as a saint with direct access to the Almighty, while she may not qualify as a curate.

Mary Stocks

Whatever women do they must do twice as well as men to be thought half so good . . . luckily, it's not difficult.

Charlotte Whitton

A woman in authority is often unpopular, only because she is efficient.

Baroness Burton of Coventry

113

To be a woman and a writer
is double mischief, for
the world will slight her
who slights 'the servile house,' and who would rather
make odes than beds.

Dilys Laing

[Women] have a right to work wherever they want to — as long as they have dinner ready when you get home.

John Wayne

A career woman who has survived the hurdle of marriage and maternity encounters a new obstacle: the hostility of men.

Caroline Bird

As soon as a woman crosses the border into male territory, the nature of professional combat changes.

Françoise Giroud

I think housework is the reason most women go to the office.

Heloise Cruse

Students of women's lives have sometimes claimed that spinsterhood and childlessness are the price such women paid for the unusual career paths they pursued. *Alice Rossi*

I have too many fantasies to be a housewife.

Marilyn Monroe

Women aren't supposed to work. They're supposed to be married. *Johnnie Tillmon*

114

Being a woman is a profession whose only patron is God.

François Truffaut

A liberated woman is one who has sex before marriage and a job after.

Gloria Steinem

In days of yore, heaven protected the working girl. Nowadays it takes a union, a wage-hour law, unemployment compensation, social security, health insurance and a pension plan.

Anon.

History

... women are not such silly giddy creatures as many proud men would make them ... Let such but look into history, they will find examples of illustrious women to confute them.

Bathsua Makin

Great women belong to history and to self-sacrifice.

Leigh Hunt

Thus far women have been the mere echoes of men. Our laws and constitutions, our creeds and codes, and the customs of social life are all of masculine origin. The true woman is as yet a dream of the future.

The prolonged slavery of women is the darkest page in human history.

Elizabeth Cady Stanton

Anyone who knows anything of history knows that great social changes are impossible without the feminine ferment. Social progress can be measured exactly by the social position of the fair sex (the ugly ones included).

Karl Marx

The happiest women, like the happiest nations, have no history.

George Eliot

The test of civilization is the estimate of woman. Among savages she is a slave. In the dark ages of Christendom she is a toy and a sentimental goddess. With increasing moral light, and larger liberty, and more universal justice, she begins to develop as an equal human being.

George William Curtis

The long historic serfdom of woman, creeping down into the moral and intellectual natures of the two sexes, has exaggerated the naturally complementary relation of the male and the female into an absurd caricature of strength on the one hand and dependence on the other.

Edward Carpenter

The history of mankind is a history of repeated injuries and usurpations on the part of man toward woman, having in direct object the establishment of a tyranny over her.

Women's Rights Convention manifesto, Seneca Falls, 1848

The history of women is the history of the worst form of tyranny the world has ever known – the tyranny of the weak over the strong. It is the only tyranny that lasts.

Oscar Wilde

117

When new-born humanity was learning to stand upright, it depended much on its mother and stood close to her protecting side. Then women were goddesses, they conducted divine worship, woman's voice was heard in council, she was loved and revered and genealogies were reckoned through her.

Maude Glasgow

The dogma of woman's complete historical subjection to men must be rated as one of the most fantastic myths ever created by the human mind.

Mary Ritter Beard

The history of men's opposition to women's emancipation is more interesting perhaps than the story of that emancipation itself.

Virginia Woolf

Like all sciences and all valuations, the psychology of women has hitherto been considered only from the point of view of men.

Karen Horney

The modern woman is the curse of the universe. A disaster, that's what. She thinks that before her arrival on the scene no woman ever did anything worthwhile before, no woman was ever liberated until her time, no woman really ever amounted to anything.

Adela Rogers St Johns

Women and revolution! What tragic, unsung epics of courage lie silent in the world's history!

Yang Ping

Like their personal lives, women's history is fragmented, interrupted, a shadow history of human beings whose existence has been shaped by the efforts and the demands of others.

Elizabeth Janeway

How did Chinese women, after having their feet bound for many generations, finally discover they could run?

Betty Friedan

It is possible that the women of the old gynocracies brought on their own downfall by selecting the phallic wild man over the more civilized men of their own pacific and gentle world.

*

[Nineteenth-century women] were a special kind of property, not quite like houses or beasts of burden, yet not quite people ... Her place in the scheme of things, if she was fortunate, was that of a household pet.

Elizabeth Gould Davis

A century and a half ago there were no knickers and girls read the Bible, now they wear impenetrable body stockings and read *Portnoy's Complaint*.

Kenneth Tynan

At this moment in history only women can (if they will) support the entry or re-entry of women into the human race.

Phyllis Chesler

Women are the only exploited group in history who have been idealised into powerlessness.

Erica Jong

Society, Politics,
and Religion

Affairs outside the home are the province of men – it is not for women to advise on them.

Aeschylus

By now you will have discovered that women too can be militant.

Sophocles

A free woman. At last free! Free from slavery in the kitchen where I walked back and forth stained and squalid among cooking pots.

Mother of Sumangala

Let your women keep silence in the churches: for it is not permitted unto them to speak.

*

If they will learn any thing, let them ask their husbands at home: for it is a shame for women to speak in the church.

Romans 14:34, 35

The judgment of God upon your sex endures even today; and with it inevitably endures your position of criminal at the bar of justice.

Do you know that each of you women is an Eve? The sentence of God on this sex of yours lives in this age; the guilt must necessarily live too. You are the gate of Hell, you are the temptress of the forbidden tree; you are the first deserter of the divine law.

Tertullian

Men have broad and large chests, and small narrow hips, and are more understanding than women, who have but small and narrow chests, and broad hips, to the end they should remain at home, sit still, keep house, and bear and bring up children.

Martin Luther

The First Blast of the Trumpet Against the Monstrous Regiment of Women.

John Knox (title of pamphlet, 1558)

Was there ever any so abused, so slandered, so railed upon, or so wickedly handled undeservedly as are we women?

Jane Anger

Were't not for gold and women, there would be no damnation.

Cyril Tourneur

A fierce beast and a dangerous foe is an outrageous woman in a Commonwealth.

R.M.

Woman, the greatest part of the lesser world, is generally become the subject of every pendanticall goose-quill. Every fantasticke Poetaster which . . . can but patch a hobling verse together, will strive to represent figments imputed to our sex . . .

Costantia Munda

I would, without a doubt, rather be a simple soldier than be a woman, because to be truthful, a soldier can become king, but a woman can never become free.

Madeleine de Scudéry

A woman ought to read and meditate on the scriptures, and regulate her conduct by them, and to keep silence, agreeably to the command of St Paul.

Anne Dacier

As the faculty of writing has been chiefly a masculine endowment, the reproach of making the world miserable has always been thrown upon the women.

Dr Johnson

One reason women are forbidden to preach the gospel, is, that they would persuade without argument and reprove without giving offence.

John Newton

Society, which greatly shrinks men, reduces women to almost nothing.

Nicolas de Chamfort

. . . as blind obedience is ever sought for by power, tyrants and sensualists are in the right when they endeavour to keep women in the dark, because the former only want slaves and the latter a play-thing.

Mary Wollstonecraft

The barbarous custom of wresting from woman whatever she possesses, whether by inheritance, donation or her own industry, and conferring it all upon the man she marries, to be used at his own discretion and will, perhaps waste it on his wicked indulgences, without allowing her any control or redress, is such a monstrous perversion of *justice* by *law*, that we might marvel how it could obtain in a Christian community.

Sarah Josepha Hale

. . . women are bought and sold in our slave markets, to gratify the brutal lust of those who bear the name of Christians.

*

I am inclined to think, when we [women] are admitted to the honor of studying Greek and Hebrew, we shall produce some various readings of the Bible a little different from those we now have.

Sarah Moore Grimké

Can man be free if woman be a slave?

Percy Bysshe Shelley

A woman has the same human nature that a man has, the same human rights — to life, liberty, and the pursuit of happiness — the same human duties; and they are as inalienable in a woman as in a man.

Theodore Parker

. . . women are the real architects of society.

Harriet Beecher Stowe

The religious superstitions of women perpetuate their bondage more than all other adverse influences.

*

The Bible and Church have been the greatest stumbling blocks in the way of women's emancipation.

*

The whole tone of Church teaching in regard to woman is, to the last degree, contemptuous and degrading.

Elizabeth Cady Stanton

For women there are, undoubtedly, great difficulties in the path, but so much the more to overcome. *Maria Mitchell*

According to the Bible, woman was the last thing God made. It must have been a Saturday night. Clearly, He was tired.

Alexandre Dumas, fils

. . . women have been called queens for a long time, but the kingdom given them isn't worth ruling. *Louisa May Alcott*

There will never be a generation of great men until there has been a generation of free women — of free mothers.

Robert G. Ingersoll

A man without religion is to be pitied, but a Godless woman is a horror above all things.

Augusta Evans

At this whole spectacle of woman's degradation the human male has looked on with stupid and open-mouthed indifference — as an ox might look on at a drowning ox-herd — not even dimly divining that his own fate was somehow involved.

Edward Carpenter

Woman was God's second mistake.

Friedrich Nietzsche

If we would know the political and moral condition of a state, we must ask what rank women hold in it. — Their influence embraces the whole of life.

A. Martien

Old-fashioned ways which no longer apply to changed conditions are a snare in which the feet of women have always become readily entangled.

Jane Addams

The labor of women in the house, certainly, enables men to produce more wealth than they otherwise could; and in this way women are economic factors in society. But so are horses.

Charlotte Perkins Gilman

We have in us the blood of a womanhood that was never bought and never sold; that wore no veil and had no foot bound; whose realized ideal of marriage was sexual companionship and an equality in duty and labour.

Olive Schreiner

Whether our reformers admit it or not, the economic and social inferiority of women is responsible for prostitution.

*

125

Now, woman is confronted with the necessity of emancipating herself from emancipation, if she really desires to be free.

*

There is no hope even that woman, with her right to vote, will ever purify politics.

Emma Goldman

There would be no adequate civilization, no Christianity, until cooperation displaced competition, and women were become equal in economic rights as they were in franchise rights.

Vernon Louis Parrington

Women who set a low value on themselves make life hard for other women.

Nellie L. McClung

No future life could heal the degradation of having been a woman. Religion in the world had nothing but insults for women.

*

It will all go on as long as women are stupid enough to go on bringing men into the world . . .

Dorothy Miller Richardson

Women's rights are men's duties.

Karl Kraus

Woman: the peg on which the wit hangs his jest, the preacher his text, the cynic his grouch, and the sinner his justification.

Helen Rowland

Women have broken many of their old chains, but they are still enmeshed in a formidable network of man-made taboos and sentimentalities, and it will take them another generation, at least, to get genuine freedom.

*

Women, as a class, believe in none of the ludicrous rights, duties and pious obligations that men are forever gabbling about.

*

Women go to church for the same reason that farmers and convicts go to church.

*

No woman is really humble; she is merely politic.

*

The way to put an end to the gaudy crimes that the suffragist alarmists talk about is to shave the heads of all the pretty girls in the world, and pluck out their eyebrows, and pull their teeth, and put them in khaki, and forbid them to wriggle on dance floors, or to wear scents, or to use lip-sticks, or to roll their eyes.

*

Women are nearly always against war in modern times, for the reasons brought forward to justify it are usually either transparently dishonest or childishly sentimental, and hence provoke their scorn.

H.L. Mencken

We are here to claim our rights as women, not only to be free, but to fight for freedom. . . . Nothing but contempt is due to those people who ask us to submit to unmerited oppression. We shall not do it.

Christabel Pankhurst

A free race cannot be born of slave mothers.

Margaret Sanger

Only those women within the confines of conventionality have freedom.

Hildric Davenport

127

The outer limitations to woman's progress are caused by the fact we are living in a man's culture.

Olga Knopf

The keeping of an idle woman is a badge of superior social status.

Dorothy L. Sayers

Women sometimes seem to share a quiet, unalterable dogma of persecution that endows even the most sophisticated of them with the inarticulate poignancy of the peasant.

Zelda Fitzgerald

Women are equal because they are not different any more.

Erich Fromm

How wrong it is for woman to expect the man to build the world she wants, rather than to set out to create it herself.

Anaïs Nin

Give women scope and opportunity, and they will be no worse than men.

Nelly Ptaschkina

They say women talk too much. If you have worked in Congress you know that the filibuster was invented by men.

Clare Boothe Luce

My advice to the women's clubs of America is to raise more hell and fewer dahlias.

William Allen White

We are all monsters, if it comes to that, we women who have chosen to be something more and something less than women.

May Sarton

You can be up to your boobies in white satin with gardenias in your hair and no sugar cane for miles, but you can still be working on a plantation.

Billie Holiday

. . . I don't for one moment believe that over the centuries some universal plot has been hatched by men to keep women in a state of servitude.

Françoise Giroud

As for Western women, it seems to me that they have often had to struggle to obtain their own rights. That did not leave much time to prove their abilities. The time will come.

Indira Gandhi

Women's chains have been forged by men, not by anatomy.

Estelle R. Ramey

The single most impressive fact about the attempt by American women to obtain the right to vote is how long it took.

Alice Rossi

The claim that American women are downtrodden and unfairly treated is the fraud of the century. *Phyllis Schlafly*

The innately logical mind of woman, her unique sense of balance, orderliness, and reason, rebels at the terrible realiza-

129

tion that justice has been an empty word, that she has been forced for nearly two millennia to worship false gods and to prostrate herself at their empty shrines.

Elizabeth Gould Davis

Every woman is a committee.

*

Women should not take to religion; they are religion.

Robin Skelton

But powerlessness is still each woman's most critical problem, whether or not she is a social activist. *Toni Carabillo*

There are two kinds of women: those who want power in the world, and those who want power in bed.

Jacqueline Bouvier Onassis

When modern woman discovered the orgasm it was (combined with modern birth control) perhaps the biggest single nail in the coffin of male dominance. *Eva Figes*

The only trouble with sexually liberating women is that there aren't enough sexually liberated men to go around.

*

We [women] are not more moral, we are only less corrupted by power. *Gloria Steinem*

... we are still the property of men, the spoils today of warriors who pretend to be our comrades in the struggle, but who merely seek to mount us. *Maria Isabel Barreno*

Where are the women to create new fictions, to go beyond inner space — as women are doing every day in real life — into the outer world of invention, action, imagination?

Molly Haskell

Women were the sacrificial lambs of the Depression, but amid the collective pain of the nation's empty bellies, they scarcely felt the knife.

*

For the Cinema Woman is a Popcorn Venus, a delectable but insubstantial hybrid of cultural distortions.   *Marjorie Rosen*

I became a feminist as an alternative to becoming a masochist.

*

... women are the true maintenance class. Society is built upon their acquiescence, and upon their small and necessary labors.

Sally Kempton

No woman would wrap herself in the flag; it is too unbecoming.

*

Here's to woman — once our superior, now our equal.

*

Women in state affairs are like monkeys in glass shops.

*

Surely God must have been disappointed in Adam: He made Eve so different.

*

131

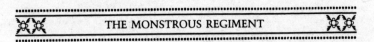

Woman's equality to man is not a claim . . . rather a concession.

Anon.

Miscellaneous

Woman, the creature of an hour.

Dante

A woman hath nine lives like a cat.

John Heywood

Every woman is a science.

John Donne

Each woman is a brief of womankind.

Sir Thomas Overbury

Better the devil's than a woman's slave.

Philip Massinger

A cat has nine lives and a woman has nine cat's lives.

Thomas Fuller

Music and women I cannot but give way to, whatever my business is.

Samuel Pepys

I must have women. There is nothing unbends the mind like them.

John Gay

He seldom errs
Who thinks the worst he can of womankind.

John Home

But what is a woman? – only one of Nature's agreeable blunders.

Hannah Cowley

Through all the drama – whether damn'd or not –
Love gilds the scene, and women guide the plot.

Richard Brinsley Sheridan

Those who always speak well of women do not know them enough: those who always speak ill of them do not know them at all.

Pigault-Lebrun

The greater part of what women write about women is mere sycophancy to man.

Germaine de Staël

The best happiness a woman can boast of is that of being most carefully deceived.

George James

If God had not created woman, he would not have created flowers.

Victor Hugo

America is the Paradise of women. That is why, like Eve, they are so extremely anxious to get out of it.   *Oscar Wilde*

Woman reduces us all to a common denominator.

George Bernard Shaw

Woman is a species of which every woman is a variety.

Arnold Haultain

A man can deceive his fiancée or his mistress as much as he likes, and, in the eyes of a woman he loves, an ass may pass for a philosopher; but a daughter is a different matter.

Anton Chekhov

And a woman is only a woman, but a good cigar is a Smoke.

Rudyard Kipling

Women and elephants never forget an injury.

Saki

The charms of a passing woman are usually in direct relation to the speed of her passing.   *Marcel Proust*

The telephone is of real use only to important businessmen or to women with something to hide.   *Colette*

Women are like elephants to me; they're nice to look at but I wouldn't want to own one.   *W.C. Fields*

Money and women are the most sought after and the least known about of any two things we have.

Will Rogers

Maybe the average Hollywood glamor-girl should be numbered instead of named.

Cecil B. De Mille

There's nothing so similar to one poodle dog as another poodle dog, and that goes for women too.

Pablo Picasso

. . . I would venture to guess that Anon, who wrote so many poems without signing them, was often a woman.

Virginia Woolf

Natural history proves it true —
Women and elephants never forget.

Dorothy Parker

Women should be obscene and not heard.

Attrib. Groucho Marx

You know even when women get into aeroplanes and fly they do not lose their liking for flowers.

Amelia Earhart

Certain women should be struck regularly, like gongs.

Noel Coward

Woman does not forget she needs the fecundator, she does not forget that everything that is born of her is planted in her.

Anaïs Nin

There are only three things to be done with a woman. You can love her, suffer for her, or turn her into literature.

Lawrence Durrell

A country is like a woman, one must not always be stuck on it.

Félix Leclerc

Women have to make jokes about themselves, laugh about themselves, because they have nothing to lose.

Agnès Varda

Women are a trouble and a worry.

Arab proverb

Women and calendars are good only for a year.

Spanish proverb

Women and hens by too much gadding are lost.

*

Women are like socks, you have to change them regularly.

*

A woman that loves to be at the window is like a bunch of grapes on the highway.

*

Women must have their wills when they live, because they make none when they die.

*

137

Women are the wildlife of a country: morality corresponds to game laws.

*

No woman is better than two.

*

A little woman is a dangerous thing.

*

If woman's actions are sometimes baffling, her motives are always obvious.

*

Woman has never created anything as beautiful as she has destroyed.

*

Women must have the last word.

Anon.

A Few Words
About Men

To famous men all the earth is a sepulchre.

Thucydides

Men willingly believe what they wish.

Julius Caesar

Do not trust men's faces.

Juvenal

They say, an old man is twice a child.

*

For these fellows of infinite tongue, that can rhyme themselves into ladies' favours, they do always reason themselves out again.

William Shakespeare

[An amorous man's] eyes are like a balance, apt to propend each way and to be weighed down with every wench's looks, his heart a weathercock, his affection tinder or naphtha itself, which every fair object, sweet smile, or mistress' favour sets on fire.

Robert Burton

Humility is a virtue all men preach, none practise, and yet everybody is content to hear.

John Selden

A man should give himself either to virtuous speech, or prudent silence.

Costantia Munda

I will not say that women are better than men, but I will say that men are not so wise as I would wish them to be . . .

Ester Sowernam

I love men, not because they are men, but because they are not women.

Queen Christina of Sweden

Could we know what Men are most apt to remember, we might know what they are most apt to do.

Lord Halifax

A nice man is a man of nasty ideas.

*

Old men and comets have been reverenced for the same reason: their long beards, and pretences to foretell events.

Jonathan Swift

The most positive men are the most credulous.

Alexander Pope

... a man that is ashamed of passions that are natural and reasonable, is generally proud of those that [are] shameful and silly.

Mary Wortley Montagu

When you have found out the prevailing passion of any man, remember never to trust him where that passion is concerned.

*

Few men can be men of pleasure, every man may be a rake.

Lord Chesterfield

Were it not for imagination, Sir, a man would be as happy in the arms of a chambermaid as of a Duchess.

*

There are few things that we so unwillingly give up, even in an advanced age, as the supposition that we still have the power of ingratiating ourselves with the fair sex.

*

Men do not suspect faults which they do not commit.

Dr Johnson

He who has no character is not a man but a thing.

Nicolas de Chamfort

He is no man who slights a woman for anything less than another woman.

Elizabeth Inchbald

141

Men, in general, are but great children.

*

There is no greater misfortune for a man than to be governed by his wife: in such a case he is neither himself nor his wife, he is a perfect nonentity.

Napoleon Bonaparte

Plausibilities and pretensions are the most direct index to the defects of men.

Sir Henry Taylor

No man speaks the truth or lives a true life two minutes together.

*

Most men are afflicted with a coldness, an incuriosity, as soon as any object does not connect with their self-love. Though they talk of the object before them, they are thinking of themselves, and their vanity is laying little traps for your imagination.

Ralph Waldo Emerson

All men who avoid female society have dull perceptions and are stupid, or else have gross tastes, and revolt against what is pure.

William Makepeace Thackeray

There is nothing that disgusts a man like getting beaten at chess by a woman.

Charles Dudley Warner

Male, *n*. A member of the unconsidered or negligible sex. The male of the human race is commonly known (to the female) as Mere Man. The genus has two varieties: good providers and bad providers.

Ambrose Bierce

142

Never trust a man who speaks well of everybody.

John Churton Collins

A man can be happy with any woman, as long as he does not love her.

*

I delight in men over seventy. They always offer one the devotion of a lifetime.

Oscar Wilde

There is such a thing as a man being too proud to fight.

Woodrow Wilson

Happiness is something men ought to pursue, although they seldom do.

George Santayana

It does not matter what the size of a man is, his vanity is just the same. A shrimp of five foot is unable to understand why a lovely goddess does not drop like a ripe peach into his mouth.

*

It is quite difficult enough to trust oneself without trusting a man!

*

To define a man: he must be a creature who makes me feel that I am a woman.

Elinor Glyn

Many a man in love with a dimple makes the mistake of marrying the whole girl.

*

The up-to-date clean-shaven snoopopathic man . . . How one would enjoy seeing a man – a real one with Nevada whiskers and long boots – land him one solid kick from behind.

Stephen Leacock

But . . . a man's sensuality is brief and seasonal and . . . its unpredictable return is never a new beginning.

Colette

Very few men care to have the obvious pointed out to them by a woman.

Margaret Baillie Saunders

I cannot recall a single masculine figure created by a woman who is not, at bottom, a booby.

*

A man's womenfolk, whatever their outward show of respect for his merit and authority, always regard him secretly as an ass, and with something akin to pity.

*

Many more men than women go insane, and many more married men than single men.

H.L. Mencken

The best way to hold a man is in your arms.

*

Give a man a free hand and he'll run it all over you.

Mae West

There are two classes of men – those who have been found out and those who have not.

*

Man clamours for, creates, controls the Magdalen – and then condemns her.

Hildric Davenport

Gentlemen prefer blondes, but marry brunettes.

Anita Loos

I require only three things of a man. He must be handsome, ruthless and stupid.

Dorothy Parker

A man goes and fights for his country, gets his inside gassed out, and loses his job, and all they give him is the privilege of marching past the Cenotaph once a year and paying four shillings in the pound income-tax.

Dorothy L. Sayers

Never trust a man with short legs – brains too near their bottoms.

Noel Coward

What most men desire is a virgin who is a whore.

Edward Dahlberg

A man who has nothing to do with women is always incomplete.

Cyril Connolly

No man can be held throughout the day by what happens throughout the night.

Sally Stanford

I never trust a man unless I've got his pecker in my pocket.

Attrib. Lyndon B. Johnson

Most men do not mature, they simply grow taller.

Leo Rosten

If men could get pregnant, abortion would be a sacrament.

Florynce R. Kennedy

You men can't stand the truth, sir, as soon as it embarrasses your interests or your pleasure . . .

Françoise Parturier

Husbands are like fires. They go out when unattended.

*

A man in love is incomplete until he has married. Then he's finished.

Zsa Zsa Gabor

No man can remove his trousers gracefully.

Robin Skelton

I refuse to consign the whole male sex to the nursery, I insist on believing that some men are my equals.

Brigid Brophy

Nothing is more debasing for a real man than a plastic apron.

Lady Lewisham

All men are rapists and that's all they are. They rape us with their eyes, their laws, and their codes.

Marilyn French

Men are those creatures with two legs and eight hands.

Jayne Mansfield

I wonder why men can get serious at all. They have this delicate long thing hanging outside their bodies, which goes up and down by its own will . . . If I were a man I would always be laughing at myself.

Yoko Ono

A gentleman is a patient wolf.

Henrietta Tiarks

A reformed rake makes the best husband.

English proverb

Men cut large thongs out of other men's leather.

Latin proverb

When a man takes a wife, he ceases to dread Hell.

Romanian proverb

Men are not to be measured by inches.

Anon.

Index

Leslie, Eliza (1787-1858) 112

Lessing, Gotthold Ephraim (1729-1781) 45

Lewisham, Lady (1929-   ) 146

Loos, Anita (1893-1981) 7, 145

Lowell, James Russell (1819-1891) 47

Luce, Clare Boothe (1903-1987) 7, 86, 128

Lugosi, Bela (1882-1956) 35

Luther, Martin (1483-1546) 1, 38, 121

Luzy, Dorothée (1747-1830) 39, 62

Lyly, John (1554?-1606) 53

Lyttelton, George, Lord (1709-1773) 30, 62

Machiavelli, Niccolò (1469-1527) 27

Makin, Bathsua (1612?-1674?) 2, 28, 116

Manner, Eeva-Liisa (1921-   ) 50, 103, 109

Mansfield, Jayne (1932-1967) 146

Margaret of Navarre (1492-1549) 71, 90

Marlowe, Christopher (1564-1593) 27

Marmion, Shackerley (1603-1639) 28, 91

Marquis, Don (1878-1937) 58

Martien, A. (fl.1875) 79, 125

Martineau, Harriet (1802-1876) 95

Marvell, Andrew (1621-1678) 92

Marx, Groucho (1895-1977) 102, 136

Marx, Karl (1818-1883) 117

Massinger, Philip (1583-1640) 133

Maugham, W. Somerset (1874-1965) 35

Maurier, George du (1834-1896) 15

Mauveaux, Julien (fl.1898) 41

McClung, Nellie L. (1873-1951) 126

McLuhan, Marshall (1911-   ) 87

Mead, Margaret (1901-1978) 86

Medici, Catherine de' (1519-1589) 38, 61

Menander (343-292 BC) 10, 70

Mencken, H.L. (1880-1956) 6, 17, 49, 58, 59, 64, 65, 69, 83, 84, 100, 101, 108, 126, 127, 144

Meredith, George (1828-1909) 48, 78

Michelet, Jules (1798-1874) 23, 56

Middleton, Thomas (1580-1627) 28

Miles, Sarah (1941-   ) 50

Milton, John (1608-1674) 2

Mitchell, Maria (1818-1889) 124

Molière, Jean Baptiste (1622-1673) 29, 92

Monroe, Marilyn (1926-1962) 114

Montagu, Mary Wortley (1689-1762) 141

Montaigne, Michel Eyquem (1533-1592) 11

Moore, Thomas (1779-1852) 56

Morata, Olimpia (1526-1555) 111

Morley, Christopher (1890-1957) 36

Morpurgo, Rahel (1790-1871) 4

Morton, Sarah Wentworth (1759-1846) 111

Mozart, Wolfgang Amadeus (1756-1791) 31

Munda, Costantia (fl.1617) 122, 140

Musset, Alfred de (1810-1857) 77

Mussolini, Benito (1883-1945) 101

Nash, Ogden (1902-1971) 36

Nathan, George Jean (1882-1958) 41

Needham, Richard J. (1912-   ) 109

Newton, John (1725-1807) 122

Nichols, Beverley 36

Nietzsche, Friedrich (1844-1900)